TIME

TALENT

ENERGY

MICHAEL MANKINS | ERIC GARTON

TIME

TALENT

ENERGY

Overcome Organizational Drag and
Unleash Your Team's Productive Power

HARVARD BUSINESS REVIEW PRESS

Boston, Massachusetts

Copyright 2017 Bain & Company
All rights reserved
Printed in the United States of America

10 9 8 7 6 5 4 3 2

RAPID® is a registered trademark of Bain & Company.
Net Promoter Score® is a registered trademark of Bain & Company, Fred Reichheld, and Satmetrix Systems, Inc.
Founder's Mentality® is a registered trademark of Bain & Company.

No part of this publication may be reproduced, stored in or introduced into a retrieval system, or transmitted, in any form, or by any means (electronic, mechanical, photocopying, recording, or otherwise), without the prior permission of the publisher. Requests for permission should be directed to permissions@hbsp .harvard.edu, or mailed to Permissions, Harvard Business School Publishing, 60 Harvard Way, Boston, Massachusetts 02163.

The web addresses referenced in this book were live and correct at the time of the book's publication but may be subject to change.

Library of Congress Cataloging-in-Publication Data

Names: Mankins, Michael C., author. | Garton, Eric (Writer on
    organizational effectiveness)
Title: Time, talent, energy : overcome organizational drag and unleash
    your team's productive power / Michael Mankins and Eric Garton.
Description: Boston, Massachusetts : Harvard Business Review Press,
    [2017] | Includes bibliographical references.
Identifiers: LCCN 2016037615 | ISBN 9781633691766
Subjects: LCSH: Organizational effectiveness. | Management. | Corporate
    culture. | Personnel management.
Classification: LCC HD58.9 .M3555 2017 | DDC 658.4/022—dc23
LC record available at https://lccn.loc.gov/2016037615

ISBN: 9781633691766
eISBN: 9781633691773

The paper used in this publication meets the requirements of the American National Standard for Permanence of Paper for Publications and Documents in Libraries and Archives Z39.48-1992.

CONTENTS

The Truly Scarce Resources

Too many companies are living in yesterday's world. They are seeking competitive advantage through traditional methods, and they aren't finding it. And they are missing their main opportunity for boosting performance and outstripping competitors.

Let us explain what we mean.

Strategy is the art and science of resource allocation. CEOs and their senior teams are ultimately responsible for setting strategy. So the hallmark of great leaders is the ability to allocate their companies' scarce resources to outpace rivals.

For most of the past fifty years, the number-one resource executives obsessed about was financial capital. Money was scarce, and those who could obtain it and put it to work most effectively were likely to come out on top. Companies such as General Electric and Berkshire Hathaway were lauded for the discipline with which they deployed their capital. The Boston Consulting Group's famous growth-share matrix put capital allocation at the heart of corporate strategy. (It advised executives to milk their companies' "cows" to fund growth in their "stars.") Even much of today's thinking about mergers and acquisitions is premised on the relative scarcity and high cost of financial capital. Overpay for your next big deal, the theory goes, and your company's shares will suffer. In short, disciplined capital management was fundamental to business success.

But today's world is different.

Financial capital is abundant and cheap. Our colleagues in the Bain Macro Trends Group estimate that total global capital has more than tripled over the past two decades and now stands at roughly ten times global GDP.[1] As capital has grown more plentiful, its price has plummeted. For many large companies, the after-tax cost of borrowing is below the rate of inflation, meaning that real borrowing costs hover close to zero. Indeed, any reasonably profitable enterprise can readily obtain the capital it needs to buy new equipment, fund new product development, enter new markets, or even acquire new businesses. To be sure, executive teams need to manage capital as carefully as ever; to do otherwise is to shoot yourself in the foot. But right now, the allocation of financial capital is no longer a source of competitive advantage.

What are today's scarce resources, the new sources of competitive advantage? For most companies, the truly scarce resources are the *time*, *talent*, and *energy* of their people, and the ideas those people generate and implement. A single great idea, after all, can put a company on top for many years—think of Apple and the iPhone, Netflix's decision to develop original content, or even the thumbs-up "like" at Facebook. Lots of smaller, everyday good ideas can enable a company to pull away from competitors. But ideas don't just materialize;

they are the product of individuals and teams who have the time to work productively, who have the skills they need to make a difference, and who bring creativity and enthusiasm to their jobs. In this era, in our brave new world of abundant and nearly free financial capital, what separates the best from the rest is leaders' ability to manage human capital in the broadest sense, meaning the people and ideas that produce results. The more talented people a company attracts, the more effectively it focuses their time on value-adding missions, and the more energy those people bring to the workplace, the higher the quality of their ideas and the quantity of the output they produce.

Just as some companies once wasted financial capital through a host of misguided or myopic moves, many of today's enterprises squander their precious time, talent, and energy, most often unintentionally. Perhaps they add new products, open up new markets, and acquire new businesses. Or they grow from a startup into a global enterprise, adding structure, professional management, checks and balances, processes, and policies along the way. But then they begin to experience what we call *organizational drag*. The complexity of their structure increases with each new product, market, and business, bloating costs and slowing decision making. Employees find themselves wasting time on needless internal interactions, unproductive or inconsequential meetings, and unnecessary e-communications. The organization gets in the way of getting things done. Not many of us can generate great ideas when we are trapped in thickets of meetings and bureaucratic procedures.

Even when a company minimizes this drag, it may deploy and team its talent in ways that undermine performance. Maybe, for instance, it spreads its top talent evenly throughout the organization rather than concentrating it where it can have the greatest impact on strategy and performance. This egalitarian approach to talent management may appear fair, even admirable, but it rarely leads to great results. It fails to take full advantage of the force multiplier that great teams can bring to idea generation and implementation.

Then there's that intangible that we think of as energy, meaning the enthusiasm and commitment that people bring to their work. A dysfunctional culture and working environment sap everyone's energy, demoralizing teams and interfering with productivity. Unless it engages most of its employees and inspires at least a few, no company can consistently generate great ideas and great performance.

The best CEOs today are great managers of these scarce resources. And just as organizations that invested financial capital more wisely than their rivals performed better in the past, the companies that do the best job of managing time, talent, and energy are the ones that win today's competitive races.

Netflix, for example, didn't get where it is just because it had a better business model than Blockbuster. It reached the top and has stayed there because it attracts, retains, and effectively utilizes many of the best people in the business. "The best thing you can do for employees—a perk better than foosball or free sushi—is hire only 'A' players to work alongside them," wrote Patty McCord, the company's chief talent officer from 1998 to 2012. "Excellent colleagues trump everything else." Netflix hires "fully formed adults," self-sufficient people "who feel responsible for the company, knowing that they will exercise discretion and responsibility." The company has no vacation policy and no travel expense policy. Nor does it have formal reviews, which it believes create unnecessary bureaucracy. Instead, Netflix fosters continuous, open, and honest conversations about performance. The strength of the company's talent has enabled Netflix to shift its business model and strengthen its leadership position over the last ten years.[2]

Or look at DaVita, a leading kidney-dialysis company that was close to bankruptcy back in 1999. A new CEO, Kent Thiry, created a culture that engages and inspires thousands of front-line employees, unleashing a torrent of energy and ideas that have reshaped how the company functions. "We are going to flip the ends and means of this business," he said early on. "We are a community first and a company second." In the DaVita community—now well into its second decade—employees are teammates or citizens and Thiry is "mayor." People who go the extra mile for patients are regularly singled out and celebrated. DaVita's "wildly spirited nationwide meeting, in which thousands of employees celebrate awards, mourn the death of patients, and connect with the emotional side of their work, is truly something to behold," observes an article in *Harvard Business Review*. Thiry makes a point of reinforcing a sense of belonging and ownership; he typically ends these meetings with the exchange, "Whose company is it?" and the audience responds, "Ours!" Since Thiry took over, DaVita's market capitalization has increased from $200 million to more than $13 billion today.[3]

Then there's Anheuser-Busch InBev (AB InBev), the giant brewer. Here is a huge company, a worldwide leader in a mature industry, exactly the kind of organization you might expect to find weighed down by bureaucracy and productivity-killing procedures. Yet CEO Carlos Brito and his leadership team have systematically focused on eliminating sources of bureaucracy and wasted time. They work around a shared table, lowering the barriers to informal, one-on-one discussion and decision making. Information does not flow up different organizational silos, to be vetted by multiple layers of executives and then reintegrated at the top; instead, everyone has quick and easy access to the data he or she needs for decisions. So it is throughout the organization. AB InBev's culture discourages internal email. It encourages face-to-face communications and small, impromptu meetings structured for discussion rather than for presentations. No surprise: at AB InBev, very little time is squandered.[4]

As these examples suggest, there is a world of difference between the top companies—those that are the best managers of time, talent, and energy—and everybody else: as we will show in chapter 1, the top quartile has over 40 percent more productive power at its disposal than the average of the bottom three quartiles. This is a huge advantage. It translates into significantly higher operating-profit margins, often 30 percent to 50 percent higher than industry averages. As this difference is compounded, the gap between the best and the rest grows bigger every year. Over a decade, the average top-quartile company has the organizational capacity to produce *more than thirty times* the output of the average company in the lower group (see figure P-1).

Most companies, unfortunately, haven't caught up to these changes. They maintain rigorous procedures for managing financial capital, as indeed they should. They set hurdle rates with care, and they require a compelling business case for any new investment. But too often they fail to manage the truly scarce resources of time, talent, and energy with equal rigor. Many are unaware of how their leaders and employees spend their hours at work. They may hire talented people, but they team and deploy those individuals ineffectively. They also fail to engage and inspire their employees, which means they get virtually none of the immense discretionary energy and

FIGURE P-1

Top-quartile companies outproduce others by more than 30 times over 10 years

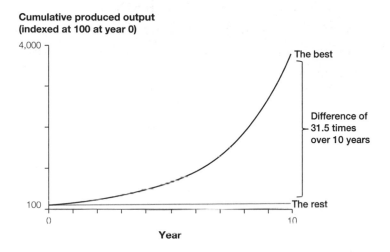

Source: Bain/EIU research (N = 308)

effort people can bring to the workplace. When they run into trouble, their first (and sometimes their only) reaction is to reduce head count, a move that itself is usually demoralizing. Their productivity suffers accordingly.

This book is about how to change all that. It's about how to manage your organization's time, talent, and energy with the same care that you apply to managing financial capital. It's about how to boost people's productivity rather than simply cutting costs. It is primarily a book for CEOs and other senior executives—the people who are ultimately responsible for allocating the scarce resources we describe. But it's also for leaders throughout the organization—leaders of business units, departments, or teams, for instance—many of whom can take steps right now to manage these resources for greater productivity. The transformations the book calls for are challenging, but the payoffs are often in the range of a 30 to 40 percent improvement in an organization's productive power. The view is very much worth the climb.

For us, the first step toward understanding these immense possibilities lay in a puzzling observation about speed, as we will see in chapter 1.

1

An Organization's Productive Power—and How to Unleash It

The common wisdom these days is that the business world is moving at lightning speed. That's certainly true in some respects. Technologies of all sorts evolve rapidly. Brash upstarts disrupt long-established businesses. The litany of examples is familiar.

But when you spend time inside the steel-and-glass offices of most large corporations, an entirely different phenomenon strikes you. Forget lightning, internet time, and all the other metaphors of speed. Here, things move *slowly*. Meetings drag on. Emails pile up unanswered. Delays are endemic, decisions postponed. To be sure, people seem impossibly busy. They stare intently at their computer screens and tap purposefully on their keyboards. They take meeting after meeting and call after call, often grabbing a quick lunch at their desks. They spend long hours in collaboration with colleagues who may be half a world away, which can mean coming in early or staying late. But their output, the actual work they get done, is far less than it should be.

Economists would point to data indicating that overall productivity growth has declined appreciably since 2007 and, in some sectors, has barely kept pace with the rate of inflation.[1] White-collar productivity is likely to be part of this sluggish trend, though we can't say for sure because nobody compiles separate statistics on office workers. But you hardly need statistics to know that something is amiss in the corporate world. Ask any executive about his or her company's workforce and you are likely to hear concerns like these:

> "We're supposed to have great people on board, but you wouldn't know it from the output we get."

> "Too much of our people's time gets wasted. Meetings, email, IM—it's crazy."

> "We hire some terrific people, but if they stick around here long enough they seem to lose their edge."

> "There's too much bureaucracy in this company—people can't get their work done."

Nor do the gripes come only from the top. Front-line employees and midlevel managers tell us that they are constantly frustrated—by their company's procedures and rules, by the endless meetings and countless emails, by the layers of management that separate them from their unit's ultimate boss and from the customer. "You can't get anything done around here" is a common refrain. There seems to be an unbridgeable gap between what people at every level think they ought to be producing and what they are actually able to do.

The few existing data points support the image of organizations mired in the mud. According to recent studies by CEB, a research and advisory firm, the time and effort required to complete many critical business tasks grew significantly between 2010 and 2015. Hiring a new employee took sixty-three days in 2015, up from forty-two days just five years earlier. Delivering an office IT project took more than ten months, up from less than nine months in 2010. Entering into a B2B sales contract took 22 percent longer than it did five years earlier. And in many cases, it's not just the amount of time that grew—the number of people required to complete these tasks increased as well.[2]

The implications for the economy are immense. Estimates by management scholars Gary Hamel and Michele Zanini suggest that corporate bureaucracy costs the US economy more than $3 trillion each year. Deriving their data from US Bureau of Labor Statistics figures, Hamel and Zanini estimate there are 12.5 million surplus supervisors bogging down the economy and sapping workforce productivity. They further estimate that there may be as many as 8.9 million "paper-pushing subordinates" carrying out chores of dubious value on behalf of these superiors. Redirecting these 21.4 million people into value-creating work could, in Hamel and Zanini's estimates, unleash $3 trillion or more in annual US GDP. Similar bureaucracy undermines the performance of the United Kingdom, Germany, and most other developed economies.[3]

Today's companies thus face a new kind of strategic threat. On the one hand, the external environment is speeding up. A fast-changing digital world presents exactly the right kind of environment for nimble upstarts to displace slow-moving incumbents. On the other hand, the metabolic rate of many incumbents is slowing down. A sluggish organization, one that can't make quick decisions and take quick actions, leaves itself unusually vulnerable, at risk of being left in the dust, outpaced by leaner, fitter, and more innovative competitors.

So here's the situation: talented people show up for work every day, but then something happens and they can't get as much done as they believe they could or should. We think of that something as organizational drag, a collection of institutional factors that interfere with productivity yet somehow go unaddressed. Organizational drag slows things down, decreasing output and raising costs. Organizational drag saps energy and drains the human spirit. Organizational drag interferes with the most capable executive's or employee's efforts, encouraging a "What's the use?" attitude. While the level varies, nearly every company we've studied loses a significant portion of its workforce's productive capacity to drag. It's time for companies to confront this productivity killer head on.

The outliers

These all-too-common observations, however, presented us with a puzzle. We knew things didn't have to be this way.

The two of us have a combined experience of nearly fifty years in consulting, much of that with Bain & Company, and we have worked with hundreds of large organizations. During that time, we have seen clients and other companies that have mastered the secrets of human-capital productivity. Like AB InBev, these companies don't let anyone waste time; on the contrary, they create all sorts of tools and procedures that cut through bureaucracy and encourage quick action. Like Netflix, they attract great people and put those people's talents to the most productive use. Like DaVita, they engage and even inspire their employees. Look at nearly any industry and you are likely to find outliers like these: Nordstrom in retail, Ford in manufacturing, Spotify and Salesforce.com in the web-based economy.

What accounts for the difference between such outliers and the rest of the pack? To find out, we embarked on a multiyear study of organizations. We conducted a series of organizational audits on twenty-five global corporations. We surveyed managers to understand what elements they believed most affected productivity at their company. We benchmarked the capabilities of each organization relative to best-in-class companies to determine whether it had the people, processes, and technology required to execute its strategy efficiently and effectively. We used people analytics, data mining, and other tools to assess how these organizations spent their collective time. We combed through calendar, email, IM, crowdsourcing, and other data, compiling and analyzing the implications for each company. We also examined external information from Gallup, Glassdoor, and other sources to understand how employees described working at their company in order to assess the level of engagement and advocacy of each company's workforce.

Parts of this research led to articles in *Harvard Business Review* and elsewhere. As far back as 2004, Michael Mankins advised senior leaders to "Stop Wasting Valuable Time" (September 2004). More recently, Michael and partners from Bain wrote about how most companies use and (sadly) squander their employees' precious time in "Your Scarcest Resource" (May 2014). Michael and others also examined the impact of teaming and deployment on productivity and performance, showing how the best companies are "Making Star Teams Out of Star Players" (January–February 2013). The popularity of these ideas with readers led to a series of digital articles for HBR, including, "Engaging Your Employees Is Good, But Don't Stop There" (December 2015). But there was more to be done: we wanted to study and quantify the overall impact of human-capital management on a company's productive power. So we commissioned the Economist Intelligence Unit, the business-to-business arm of The Economist Group, to mount a survey of more than three hundred executives from large companies worldwide.

The survey probed deep into people's assessments of their companies' practices. We started with basic questions, such as, "How many hours a week does the average employee in your organization work?" and "On average, how much work is conducted via teleconference and/or video conference?" Then we asked our respondents to diagnose their organization's strengths and weaknesses: "How much of your organization's productive power is lost due to inadequate employee skills, poor teaming and deployment, or lackluster leadership?" "How much is lost to insufficient automation or ineffective collaboration?" "What differences in productivity do you notice between employees who are merely satisfied and those who seem truly engaged or inspired?" We also asked respondents to share the best practices they had put in place to improve workforce productivity. We then compared the survey results with the experiences of our clients over the last thirty years.

It's the organization

If we were to sum up the premise of this book in a few sentences, they would read something like this: It's not your employees' fault that they are not as productive as they could or should be; it's your organization's fault. Workforce productivity is primarily an organizational problem and so requires organizational solutions. Unless companies identify and remove the organizational obstacles to getting things done, they will never generate great results.

To understand what this means, start with the basics. An organization is a collection of individuals with unique skills and talents. It is also a collection of hours, meaning the time that these individuals devote to the company. Both of these resources are inherently scarce. Talent? Warm bodies are readily available, but talented leaders are hard to find and a skilled workforce can take decades to assemble. Time is in even shorter supply, since no amount of money can buy a twenty-five-hour day. As for energy—the dedication, focus, and creativity each employee brings to every hour he or she spends at work—demoralized or frustrated employees, people who feel they are spinning their wheels, don't bring much energy. Those who feel they can accomplish great things typically bring a lot. The more energy people bring to the workplace, the higher the quality of output they produce.

Taken together, the three factors—time, talent, and energy—determine an organization's productive power, its ability to generate output from a given number of people. What the outlying companies have learned is this: you have to *manage* all those resources to produce great results. This task is different from simply hiring good people or keeping a lid on head count, because an organization is far more than individuals performing specific tasks according to some predetermined timetable. Unleashing the productive power of a company's workforce requires looking at the totality of the organization. You wouldn't invest your financial capital without an overall plan and without analysis that shows you how each investment fits into that plan. So it is with human and organizational capital: you have to look at the big picture. And you have to invest in a way that helps to change the entire organization rather than slapping a bandage on this or that aspect of the problem.

As intuitive as this approach to performance may be, nobody really thinks about it this way. Most of the research and writing on output and productivity focuses on actions individual employees can take to improve their personal productivity, or on steps companies can take to improve efficiency. Much of this advice is helpful, but its effects are often circumscribed by the organization. Employees are coached to copy the habits of highly effective people, for instance, but they're typically told very little about how to make these practices work when they run counter to the habits of the organization. Executives learn to restructure and reengineer in order to improve efficiency, but they don't learn how to change the cultural factors that often have a bigger impact on output than the processes themselves. And, of course, talent management gets a lot of attention. But many common techniques for identifying, appraising, developing, deploying, and teaming difference-making talent are rooted in out-of-date human resources practices that have failed to deliver the intended results. Frustrated with these tools, some executives have led a backlash, reflected in a slew of articles explaining "why we love to hate HR." But what's left has an "execute or execute" flavor to it. When a star player fails to accomplish a herculean business goal, overcoming any number of organizational obstacles, executives are advised to replace the failure with someone who can get the job done.

Quantifying the possibilities

The survey research enabled us to create a quantitative model of three critical concerns: how much productive power companies lose to organizational drag; to what extent they can compensate for that deficit through astute talent management; and how much productive capacity can be further enhanced by tapping into the discretionary energy of their workforce. This allowed us to assess the gap between the most successful companies and their average-performing peers. The model shows the big picture that we think organizations need to consider. It also allows us to estimate the numerical effects of the various factors that come into play, thereby assessing whether it's really worthwhile to invest in changing things. To be sure, the data is based on self-reported estimates and so must be treated with some care. But the survey numbers generally fit closely with estimates based on our own experience. They also match specific productivity studies conducted by our colleagues at Bain and by our clients. And they certainly indicate the orders of magnitude that a company has to deal with as it considers reshaping its organization to unleash workforce productivity.

So here's what we found, in broad terms:

Organizational drag wastes time and undermines productivity. The average company loses more than 20 percent of its productive power to organizational drag—all the practices, procedures, and structures that waste time and limit output. Organizational drag is an inevitable and sometimes invisible force that slows the metabolic rate of a company and affects its health. It's a chronic illness like high blood pressure—

you have to manage it all the time or it will get the best of you. Because of organizational drag, most companies have a productivity deficit. They produce far less than they could or should.

This deficit may in fact be significantly more than 20 percent. In our work with clients, for example, we typically find that 25 percent or more of the typical line supervisor's time is wasted *just in unnecessary meetings or e-communications.* If you're that supervisor, you're spending more than a day a week doing nothing but needless interaction. You're in meetings that should never have been scheduled or that you shouldn't have been invited to. You're responding to emails that should never have been sent or that shouldn't have reached your inbox.

Good talent management can compensate for some of the productivity that's lost to organizational drag. As if acting on instinct, companies often try to make up for lost productive power by hiring, developing, and retaining better talent, and by deploying that talent in ways that boost productivity. But we found that the typical company makes up less than half the productive power lost to organizational drag through talent management alone.

Of course, great talent—the individual who is significantly more skilled or inspirational than others—is much more productive than average or mediocre talent. So it isn't surprising that the top companies we studied have a slightly better-than-average mix of great people. Beyond the raw mix, however, we found that the best-performing companies focused their best talent in a few critical roles. In essence, these companies have more "difference makers" *and* they assign these exceptional individuals to roles where they will have the biggest impact on the company's performance.

The most productive companies are also far more disciplined in how they assemble and deploy teams. They aren't afraid to create all-star teams when they're confronted with mission-critical initiatives. They take steps to ensure that all of their teams can collaborate efficiently and effectively to get things done. In short, the outliers recognize that teaming is *more* important than simply bringing in great talent, because most work gets done in teams.

Employee engagement and inspiration can make up more of the lost productivity. Most companies have tried hard to engage their employees. Some have even set out to inspire their workers. This is how companies hope to release the discretionary energy people bring to work.

And it's true: these steps can often have a tremendous impact on productivity. Our research suggests that an employee who is satisfied with his or her work is 40 percent more productive than an unsatisfied one. But an engaged employee is 44 percent more productive than a satisfied worker, and an employee who feels inspired at work is nearly 125 percent more productive than a satisfied one. In short, an organization would need about two-and-a-quarter satisfied employees to produce as much as a single inspired worker. The higher the percentage of engaged and inspired employees in your organization's workforce, the higher its productive power.

As we noted, time, talent, and energy taken together explain an organization's productive power. But companies concerned with their organization will have to face a sad truth: all but the very best companies lose so much of their productive power to organizational drag that they can only just make up for the loss through talent management and employee engagement.

The productive power index

To understand the magnitudes involved, it helps to think of an organization's productive power as an index. We assume that a company starts with 100—the output it should produce with an average mix of largely satisfied employees who can devote 100 percent of their time to productive work. That's the top line in figure 1-1.

From this base of 100, we subtract the productive power lost to organizational drag—all the factors that waste time and prevent employees from being as productive as they could be. That's the next line in figure 1-1. As you can see, the average company loses 21 percent of its productive power to organizational drag. The index plunges to 79.

Now let's add the gains (or losses) that organizations realize from their mix of talent, collaboration practices, and

FIGURE 1-1

The average company barely offsets organizational drag through its talent and energy

Productive Power Index: Companies in the Bottom Three Quartiles (%)

Productive capacity	**+100**
Time (Drag)	**-21**
Talent	**+10**
Energy	**+24**
Productive output	**=113**

Source: Bain/EIU research

20

approaches to teaming and deployment. The average company gains back 10 points on the index from talent management, bringing the index score up to 89.

Finally, we add (or subtract) the productivity impact of having more (or less) satisfied, engaged, and inspired employees. This is a powerful factor: the average company gains another 24 points from its employees' level of engagement. Even so, look at the overall result. On an indexed basis, the average company barely pokes its head above water. Its productive power index stands at 113, compared to a starting point of 100.

Now let's examine the difference between the best companies—the top quartile in our survey sample—and the rest, meaning the average of the remaining three quartiles. That gap is stunning, and it's a good indication of how top players like Netflix or AB InBev outstrip the competition by running a better organization.

Look closely at the upper graphic in figure 1-2. Using the same procedure as in figure 1-1, we calculate the effects of organizational drag, talent management, and the energy generated by the companies' levels of engagement and inspiration. As the graph shows, the bottom three quartiles in our sample manage time, talent, and energy to generate a productive power index of just 102. Talented people come in the door, sure. But the organization drags them down, and the companies' leaders can't compensate either through better talent management or through higher levels of engagement and inspiration.

But the top quartile is quite different, as shown in the lower graphic in the same figure. Companies in this group lose far less to organizational drag, only 13 points as compared to 24 for the other three quartiles. They also make up far more of that loss through talent and energy. These companies have better people. They team and deploy those people more effectively,

FIGURE 1-2

The best versus the rest

Productive Power Index: Companies in the Bottom Three Quartiles (%)

Productive capacity	**+100**	STARTING POWER INDEX
Time (Drag)	**–24**	
Talent	**+4**	
Energy	**+22**	
Productive output	**=102**	ADJUSTED POWER INDEX

Productive Power Index: Companies in the Top Quartile (%)

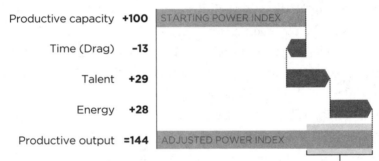

Productive capacity	**+100**	STARTING POWER INDEX
Time (Drag)	**–13**	
Talent	**+29**	
Energy	**+28**	
Productive output	**=144**	ADJUSTED POWER INDEX

The best can produce 1.4 times as much with the same resources, and this difference compounds every year.

Source: Bain/EIU research

and they foster better collaboration. They also engage and inspire employees to invest more of their discretionary energy in the company's success. That's how they generate a productive power index of 144, or over 40 percent more than the average of the other three quartiles.

In short, the best companies are nearly half again as productive as the rest, purely as a result of the way they manage their organization's scarcest resources—time, talent, and energy. These companies get more work done by lunchtime Thursday than the rest accomplish all week, and with higher quality. They don't have to worry about cutting head count to boost efficiency, simply because they are so productive. They outpace the competition year after year. The size of the prize is enormous.

How productive is your organization?

This diagnostic test will help you create a quick qualitative assessment of your organization's productive power, along with the factors that most affect it. It is not intended to be an in-depth assessment of time, talent, and energy, only an indicator. For a full diagnostic of your company, please visit our website: www.timetalentenergy.com.

TIME

The term "productive output" as defined here means work conducted by employees to advance specific objectives that produce business results. If employees were to work productively and efficiently for 100 percent of their time, they would generate productive output of 100 percent. In reality, an employee typically faces constraints that impinge on 100 percent efficiency. Several factors that can cause loss of productive output are:

- Employees lack sufficient direction to know what to do.

- Employees lack the skills and capabilities required to best do their work.

- The organization lacks the systems, processes, and tools to enable people to do their work efficiently.

- The organizational structure gets in the way and results in work taking more time than it should (e.g., bureaucracy and hierarchy).

- People work together in ways that are inefficient and ineffective (e.g., poorly managed meetings).

- The culture leads people to work on tasks that do not advance a specific business outcome and/or do not produce business results (e.g., a culture of overprepared-ness, excessive stakeholder management, or risk aversion).

- People are not satisfied with their job or the workplace and therefore do not devote their energy and attention to doing their work efficiently and effectively.

- Other.

  1. How many of the factors listed do you experience at your organization?

     a. 0 or 1 factors

     b. 2 or 3 factors

     c. 4 or more factors

  2. On average, how many hours do you or members of your team spend in meetings each day?

     a. Less than 3 hours

     b. Between 3 and 6 hours

     c. More than 6 hours

3. How many layers of management are there between front-line employees and the CEO at your organization?

    a. Fewer than 6 layers

    b. Between 6 and 8 layers

    c. More than 8 layers

TALENT

Talent refers to the capabilities of the people in the organization, how they are deployed, and how they are teamed. Please answer the following questions with white-collar workers in mind.

4. What percentage of your workers are high performers or "A-level" talent (that is, among the very best available in their industry or field, not just in your company)?

    a. More than 25 percent

    b. 10 percent to 25 percent

    c. Less than 10 percent

5. How effective is your organization at identifying the company's difference makers and placing them in roles where they can make the greatest difference?

    a. We are great at identifying the difference makers and placing them in mission-critical roles.

    b. We know who the difference makers are and which roles are mission critical, but we don't always get the right people in the right roles.

    c. We lack the processes to identify difference-making talent or we don't have a clear articulation of the mission-critical roles.

6. In your experience, when your organization has launched a new initiative that was critical to business success, how has it approached forming a team to drive the initiative?

   a. The organization generally creates a team made up entirely or predominantly of high performers.

   b. We typically pick a high performer to lead the team and let the rest fall into place.

   c. The organization generally creates teams composed of people who were available.

ENERGY

Energy refers to whether people are engaged and inspired by their job, the organization they work for, and the people they work with, and is reflected in how much they are willing to contribute to their company. Please answer the following questions with white-collar workers in mind.

7. What percentage of your organization's employees are "inspired"? Inspired people are those who, because of their work, the company's purpose, and the relationships with the people they work with, are vocal advocates for the company and are committed to doing extraordinary things to contribute to it.

   a. More than 50 percent

   b. 25 percent to 50 percent

   c. Less than 25 percent

8. Does your organization have a culture that drives both performance and engagement?

   a. Yes, our culture effectively drives both performance and engagement.

b. Our culture drives performance or engagement but not both in equal measure.

c. No, our culture does not effectively drive performance or engagement.

9. Does your organization have a formal program to help employees become inspirational leaders?

a. Our organization provides significant leadership development, including inspirational leadership.

b. Our organization provides leadership development but does not emphasize inspirational leadership.

c. Our organization provides limited formal leadership development.

SCORING

Tally up your scores. All "A" answers receive 2 points, "B" answers receive 1 point, and "C" answers receive 0 points.

- 14 to 18 points: High. Your organization is likely a high performer on time, talent, and energy. We encourage you to review which area you scored lowest in and use this book to amplify your already high performance.

- 7 to 13 points: Medium. Your organization is likely an average performer on time, talent, and energy and may be losing 20 percent to 30 percent of its productive power compared to the best performers.

- 0 to 6 points: Low. Your organization is likely losing considerable productive power, up to 40 percent compared to the best performers.

Take note of your overall score and your score for each component of time, talent, and energy. Where is your organization the weakest? Where is it the strongest? The component with the lowest score is potentially the most valuable lever for initial attempts at improving your organization, but making incremental changes to your strong areas can also deliver significant value.

What you'll find in this book

All these statistics can sound pretty theoretical. But the chapters that follow will put flesh on the numerical bones.

Part One is about managing time, because if you don't manage time well, you can't do anything else. Chapters 2 and 3 trace the sources of organizational drag—all those meetings, all that e-communication, all those complex bureaucratic structures. They describe in detail how companies can manage their time better, how they can streamline their operations, and how they can rid themselves of the most common impediments to productivity. They will also share the practices that leading companies implement to liberate unproductive time. Follow these prescriptions and you'll already be ahead of the pack.

Part Two focuses on talent and teaming—the second piece of the puzzle. Chapters 4 and 5 explore the power of effective talent management. You'll get some new ideas on attracting, developing, and retaining the great people any organization needs. We'll describe how to determine where your organization needs better people—"difference makers"—in order to produce great performance. You'll also learn what seems to be hidden from too many organizations—the tremendous effect of great teaming and collaboration—and how to tap into its power. Hint: it's all about where and how you deploy these difference makers.

Part Three turns to the last factor that determines an organization's productive power: that sometimes squishy issue of discretionary energy. Chapters 6 and 7 take a hard-nosed look at the power (and limits) of engagement, and at the remarkable effects of inspiration. They describe the practical steps companies can take to inspire their employees, and they examine why those seemingly practical moves so often fail. The chapters also discuss that elusive concept of culture, which in some of the outliers seems to make all the difference. Culture isn't just part of the game, as former IBM CEO Lou Gerstner once wrote; it is the game. Our research and experience support this assertion.

Taken together, the actions we describe in these chapters are self-reinforcing and self-amplifying. Once built, an engaged and productive workforce becomes a company's army of advocates to customers and to prospective employees. You're essentially creating a virtuous circle: high levels of engagement make it easier to attract and retain great talent; better talent makes it easier to assemble skilled teams; these individuals and teams put pressure on the organization to simplify its structure and eliminate the time sinks that eat up their hours. When companies liberate people's discretionary energy in this way, work seems to have more purpose. An organization that accomplishes that feat doesn't just perform well; it soars.

A few outliers have already unleashed the productive power of their organizations in just this way. They have learned to manage their people's time, talent, and energy every bit as closely as they manage financial capital, and so they are leaders in today's economy. This book will show you how to join them at the head of the pack.

THE THREE KEY POINTS
OF THIS BOOK

1. *Organizational drag is a killer.* It costs the typical company at least 20 percent of its productive capacity, probably considerably more. So you're already producing less than you could be, right from the start.

2. *Good talent management is the first step toward overcoming it.* You need great people—"difference makers"—in key positions in your organization. But the way you team and deploy your people is even more important.

3. *Engagement and especially inspiration can make your company unstoppable.* That's what releases the discretionary energy of your employees and creates true high-performance organizations.

PART ONE

TIME

Time is the scarcest resource, and unless it is
managed nothing else can be managed.

—Peter Drucker

Peter Drucker's dictum echoes through the halls of the corporate world every day. "There's never enough time." "Sorry, I don't have the time." If someone really could invent a twenty-five-hour day, he or she would make a fortune.

We use the term *organizational drag* to describe all the ways in which an organization eats up people's time. It's the meetings, the emails and phone calls, the bureaucratic processes and procedures. Some of these are essential. Others are pure time wasters. As our research shows, this kind of drag can be a killer. The average company loses 21 percent of its productive power, the equivalent of a day a week, to drag. Even the top-quartile companies lose 13 percent.

And is that really all? We asked our survey respondents, in effect, how many hours they spent in *unnecessary* meetings and communications, and they gave us their best estimate. Look at things a little more closely, however, and you realize that most people have come to view many of the meetings and communications they suffer through every day as a *necessary* part of their job. Only when their company begins managing its time more closely do they come to see that all those interactions weren't really necessary at all. They then find themselves with a whole lot more extra time than the 21 percent or 13 percent figures might suggest.

So we take a two-part approach in this section of the book. Chapter 2 examines where the time goes and how companies can get much of it back through some simple time-management tools and techniques. Chapter 3 peels back the onion to reveal the needlessly complex structures that usually underlie all those meetings and interactions. Sometimes changing these structures is a big deal, but not always. Say, for instance, that your account representatives have to interact with a dozen internal people—product managers, technology specialists, regional marketers, and so on—every time they prepare a proposal for a client, just because of the way your company is structured. If you could reshape the organization to reduce those interactions by half, you would free up countless hours of unproductive time.

You may find the stories we tell a bit startling. We'll introduce you to the meeting that ate up 300,000 hours of corporate time, most of it wasted. We'll show how an executive assistant at one company was regularly spending millions of dollars of the company's money every year, with no formal approval process. We'll describe the company that realized it didn't really need dozens of business units, hundreds of subsidiary companies, and no fewer than forty-nine corporate committees. We'll also explain why companies seem to conduct those familiar spans-and-layers analyses year after year, without much effect on productivity. But for every cautionary tale, there's a more inspiring one, of companies that have finally learned to manage their time effectively—and have the results to show for it.

Read on. Time's a-wasting.

2

Liberate the Organization's Time

As we noted earlier, most companies have elaborate procedures for managing financial capital: business cases, hurdle rates, spending limits, and so on. An organization's time, by contrast, goes largely unmanaged. Although phone calls, emails, instant messages, meetings, and teleconferences eat up hours of every executive's day, companies have few rules to govern these interactions. Most companies have no clear understanding of how their leaders and employees are spending their collective time. Not surprisingly, that time is often squandered—on long email chains, needless conference calls, and countless unproductive meetings.

This lack of management results in acute organizational drag. Time devoted to internal meetings and communications detracts from time spent providing value to customers. Organizations become bloated, bureaucratic, and slow, and their financial performance suffers. Former Intel CEO Andy Grove once wrote, "Just as you would not permit a fellow employee to steal a piece of office equipment, you shouldn't let anyone walk away with the time of his fellow managers."[1] Of course, such thievery happens all the time, usually unintentionally. Meetings creep onto the calendar with no clear plan or priority. New initiatives crop up every day, demanding management attention. And the flood of messages never stops. According to our survey, executives work an average of over forty-seven hours a week—somewhat more in the Asia-Pacific region, slightly less in Europe, the Middle East, and Africa—but often have much less to show for all that effort than they would like.

What can be done? Most advice on managing time focuses on individual actions. The time gurus advise us to reassert control over our email, be far more selective about which meetings we attend, and so on. Such recommendations are worthwhile and helpful, but organizational drag can't be countered by individual actions alone: even the best time-management intentions are likely to be overwhelmed by the demands and practices of the organization. The emails and IMs keep coming. So do the meeting invitations. Ignore too many and you risk alienating your coworkers or your boss. And if this steady stream of interactions is how your company gets its work done, you have little choice about the matter: you have to plunge in and try to swim your way to the other side as best you can.

Fortunately, some of the outliers have identified ways to manage organizational time quite differently. They not only simplify *where* the work is done—by what level, which function, which business units, and so on—as we will describe in the following chapter; they also simplify *how* the work is done, saving enormous amounts of time. They expect their leaders to treat time as a scarce resource and to invest it prudently. They bring as much discipline to their companies' time budgets as they do to their capital budgets. These organizations have significantly lowered their overhead expenses. They have also liberated as much as 40 percent of unproductive time for executives and employees. That burst in productivity fuels innovation and accelerates profitable growth—and it frees employees from the frustrating, mind-deadening feeling that they are forever wasting their time.

By the numbers: how organizational time is squandered

To see how things got so bad, consider a seemingly innocent piece of technological wisdom known as Metcalfe's Law. Robert Metcalfe—at this writing a professor at the University of Texas—is a giant in the technological field, coinventor of Ethernet technology, and cofounder of 3Com, a company later acquired by Hewlett-Packard. Along the way, he formulated a rule of thumb regarding the value of any network.

Metcalfe postulated that the value of a network increases with the square of the number of network users. One fax machine, for example, is worthless. Two fax machines are worth only a little. But a network that includes thousands of fax machines is worth millions, because now all those people can send documents to one another.

Metcalfe's Law, however, has a dark side: as the cost of communications decreases, the number of interactions increases exponentially, as does the time required to process these interactions. Once upon a time, when executives or managers received a phone call while they were away, they received messages on pink slips of paper from their secretaries saying that someone had called. A busy exec might receive as many as twenty on an average day, or about five thousand a year. Then came single-user voicemail, followed by multiuser voicemail (the pre-email version of "Reply All"); the cost of leaving a message thus declined, and the number of messages left rose accordingly, perhaps to ten thousand a year. Then, finally, came today's layers of networks—phone, email, IM, and so on—in which the cost of communicating with one person or many hundreds of people is virtually nil. Not surprisingly, the number of messages has burgeoned, perhaps to fifty thousand a year (see figure 2-1). Taking, responding to, and dealing with the consequences of all those messages obviously puts a burden on the individual. But it's not only the people directly concerned whose time is consumed. Other employees must also get involved. The more senior an executive, the more time others will have to spend filtering, organizing, and coping with those fifty thousand messages and conversations.

Today, companies have time-tracking tools that weren't available in the past. With the widespread use of Microsoft Outlook, Google Calendar, Apple Calendar, and other

FIGURE 2-1

The dark side of Metcalfe's Law

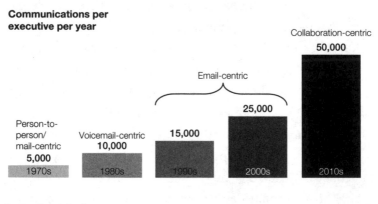

Communications per executive per year

Source: Bain & Company

enterprisewide calendar and messaging applications, companies can track where managers and employees are spending the organization's collective time and, thus, investing this scarce resource. The calendar data shows how many meetings and of what type are occurring each week, month, or year. It shows how many people are attending these sessions, by level and function within the organization. It even permits organizations to track certain organizational behaviors, such as parallel processing and double-booking, that occur before, during, and after meetings. Of course, a company scrutinizing all this data needs strong safeguards to protect employee privacy; nobody wants the feeling that Big Brother is watching his every move. But the information can paint a vivid and revealing picture of an organization's time budget.[2]

To study the use of time, we and our colleagues at Bain employed innovative people analytics tools from a Seattle-based company called VoloMetrix, which, in late 2015, became a subsidiary of Microsoft. Here's what we discovered from examining the time budgets of seventeen large corporations:

Companies are awash in e-communications. As the incremental cost of one-to-one and one-to-many communications has declined, the number of interactions has radically multiplied. Some executives now receive some two hundred emails a day, or about fifty thousand messages a year in email alone. The increasing use of IM and crowdsourcing applications promises to compound the problem. If the trend is left unchecked, executives will soon be spending more than one day of every week just managing electronic communications.

Meeting time has skyrocketed. People are also attending more meetings. There are two primary reasons. First, the cost of organizing meetings has dropped dramatically. Think about the effort that used to be involved in scheduling a meeting with five executives twenty-five years ago. To find a time, one executive's secretary had to propose a time to each of the other executives' assistants. After a series of back-and-forth communications, a date, time, and location were finally agreed on. It took a lot of effort, so executives requested far fewer meetings. Second, the number of meetings has increased because it's far easier than in the past for attendees to take part via telephone, videoconferencing, screen sharing, and the like. This has further reduced the cost associated with holding a meeting.

The result is indisputable: on average, senior executives devote more than two days every week to meetings involving three or more coworkers. Overall, about 15 percent of an organization's collective time is spent in meetings—a percentage that has increased every year since 2008.

These gatherings don't just proliferate; they cascade. A single meeting at the top can produce ripple effects throughout the organization that consume significant time and money. At one large industrial company we worked with recently, the senior leadership team held weekly meetings to review performance across the business. Those meetings directly consumed seven thousand hours a year of organizational time. In addition, each member of the leadership team met with his or her unit to prepare for the weekly meetings, consuming an additional twenty thousand hours a year. Each unit, in turn, looked to its teams to generate and cross-check critical information, mostly in meetings. These second-order effects ate up another sixty-three thousand hours a year. Finally, email and data collection extended far beyond the people involved in preparatory meetings. All told, those senior leadership meetings accounted for more than three hundred thousand hours a year (see figure 2-2).[3]

FIGURE 2-2

Ripple effects of a single leadership meeting

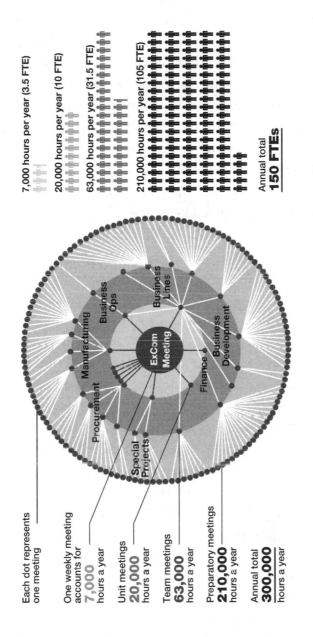

Each dot represents one meeting

One weekly meeting accounts for
7,000 hours a year

Unit meetings
20,000 hours a year

Team meetings
63,000 hours a year

Preparatory meetings
210,000 hours a year

Annual total
300,000 hours a year

7,000 hours per year (3.5 FTE)

20,000 hours per year (10 FTE)

63,000 hours per year (31.5 FTE)

210,000 hours per year (105 FTE)

Annual total
150 FTEs

Source: Michael C. Mankins, Chris Brahm, and Greg Caimi, "Your Scarcest Resource," *Harvard Business Review,* May 2014.

Real collaboration is limited. Although the number of one-to-one and one-to-many interactions has risen dramatically over the past two decades, up to 80 percent of the interactions we reviewed took place within departments, not between businesses, across functions, or between headquarters and other parts of the company. As for the interactions that did extend beyond an individual unit, analysis of their content suggests that many of them involved the wrong people or took place for the wrong reason—that is, they were primarily for information only, rather than to gather input or brainstorm alternatives. In short, more time spent interacting has not produced significantly more collaboration outside organizational silos.

Dysfunctional meeting behavior is on the rise. Meeting participants at most of the organizations we examined routinely sent emails during meetings. In 22 percent of one company's meetings, participants sent three or more emails, on average, for every thirty minutes of meeting time. (Numerous other studies have documented extensive web surfing and other distractions during teleconferences, an increasingly common way of conducting meetings. Such distractions have been shown to cause a ten-point fall in a person's IQ—the same as losing a night of sleep, or twice the effect of smoking marijuana.) At the same company, executives commonly double-booked meetings and decided later which one they would attend. So meeting organizers could never be sure whether required attendees would actually show up.

Dysfunctional behaviors like these create a vicious circle: parallel processing and double-booking limit the effectiveness of meeting time, so the organization sets up more meetings to get the work done. Those meetings prompt more dysfunctional behavior, and on and on.

Formal controls are rare. At most companies, no real costs are associated with requesting coworkers' time. If you want a meeting, your assistant merely sends out a meeting request or finds and fills an opening in the team's calendar. If you identify a problem in need of fixing, you convene a task force to study it and, most likely, launch an initiative to address it. Such demands on the organization's time typically undergo no review and require no formal approval. For example, leaders at one large manufacturing company recently discovered that a regularly scheduled ninety-minute meeting of midlevel managers cost more than $15 million annually. When asked "Who is responsible for approving this meeting?" the managers were at a loss. "No one," they replied. "Tom's assistant just schedules it and the team attends." In effect, a junior vice president's administrative assistant was permitted to invest $15 million without supervisor approval. No such thing would ever happen with the company's financial capital.

There are few consequences. In a recent Bain survey, senior executives rated more than half the meetings they attended as "ineffective" or "very ineffective." Yet few organizations have established mechanisms for assessing the productivity of individual gatherings, not to mention clear penalties for unproductive sessions or rewards for particularly valuable ones.

Think about the effect of all this on the typical entry-level manager's week. She spends roughly twenty-one hours in meetings, plus another eight dealing with e-communications. Some portion of this time is wasted on emails, calls, and IMs that should never have been sent or that she should never have responded to. More is wasted on meetings that should never have been held or that she should never have attended. If all the e-communications and meetings were bunched up at the beginning of the week, she wouldn't be able to start other work until late Thursday afternoon. But, of course, they aren't bunched up—they regularly interrupt the manager's other work. If you were to deduct periods of less than twenty minutes of working time from her productive time, you would find that she has something like 6.5 hours a week of uninterrupted time for tasks other than meetings and communications (see figure 2-3). Studies have shown that, while multitasking can be emotionally satisfying because you feel busy and important, your performance drops significantly.

The good news, however, is that between 25 percent and 40 percent of the typical manager's time is potentially recoverable. The secret is to bring greater discipline to time management.

FIGURE 2-3

Meeting overload leaves little time to think or work

Example: 40% of time can be liberated by reducing meeting frequency, reducing invitees, and/or reducing email.

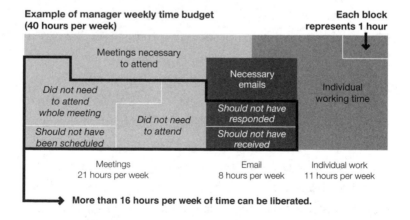

Example of manager weekly time budget (40 hours per week)

Each block represents 1 hour

Meetings necessary to attend

Did not need to attend whole meeting

Should not have been scheduled

Did not need to attend

Necessary emails

Should not have responded

Should not have received

Individual working time

| Meetings 21 hours per week | Email 8 hours per week | Individual work 11 hours per week |

More than 16 hours per week of time can be liberated.

Source: Bain & Company

How to manage your organization's time

Some Swedish companies are trying out a radically simple way to manage organizational time: give people less of it. "In Sweden, the six-hour workday is becoming common," reports the magazine *Fast Company*. One company, an app developer called Filimundus, made the switch in 2014 with no loss of productivity. The reason? "The leadership team just asked people to stay off social media and personal distractions, and eliminated some standard weekly meetings."[4]

How simple! But Sweden has long been something of an exception, and companies in other countries aren't likely to adopt the six-hour day anytime soon. Still, there are plenty of other ways to reduce organizational drag by better managing work time. These methods fall into three broad headings.

I. Invest time as carefully as you invest money

Since no company that we know of has a chief time officer, the responsibility for setting time-investment standards falls to the CEO. And some have shouldered that responsibility in innovative ways.

Be ruthless in setting priorities. When Steve Jobs was leading Apple, he would take the company's top one hundred executives off-site for a planning retreat, where he pushed them to identify the company's top ten priorities for the coming year. Members of the group competed intensely to get their ideas on the short list. Then Jobs liked to take a marker and cross out the bottom seven. "We can only do three," he would announce. His gesture made it clear what the executives should and should not focus on.[5]

Of course, you don't have to be as dramatic as Jobs. When Gary Goldberg became CEO at Newmont Mining in March 2013, he found that eighty-seven initiatives were under way across the company, each demanding the time and attention of one or more members of Newmont's executive leadership team (ELT). Many of those initiatives, including efforts to improve mine safety or increase operational efficiency, were valuable. Others were more questionable in terms of Newmont's return on investment.

To gain control over initiative creep, Goldberg insisted that leaders develop formal business plans for all the company's current and proposed initiatives. Before investing any time in an initiative, the ELT had to review the business case and approve the effort. Each plan had to specify the precise economic benefit the initiative would deliver and also its total cost, including the time of executive leaders. Every initiative was required to have an executive sponsor, who was accountable for managing its progress and keeping it on budget.

These requirements had the desired effect. Many of the initiatives that had been under way when Goldberg took over were discontinued because no one presented a business case for them. Others did go through a business-case review but were not approved. After less than three months, Newmont had scaled back the number of initiatives by one-third. Newmont also reduced the size of its corporate headquarters by 30 percent, pushing greater authority and accountability to leaders at its mine sites. And it refocused its collective time on improving safety and operational efficiency.

Create a fixed time budget—and reduce it wherever possible. Another great tool: establish a fixed amount of time for meetings and other distractions. Companies that do this say, in effect, "We will invest no additional organizational time in meetings; we will fund all new meetings through withdrawals from our existing meeting bank." As with financial budgets, these companies can then find ways to cut the time budget.

That's essentially what Alan Mulally did. When Mulally became Ford's CEO, in 2006, he discovered that the company's most senior executives spent a lot of time in meetings. In fact, the top thirty-five executives assembled every month for what they called "meetings week"—five days devoted to discussing auto programs and reviewing performance. The direct and indirect costs of these sessions were significant—far more than the company could afford at the time.

So in late 2006, Mulally asked his team to assess the efficiency and effectiveness of the company's regular meetings. The team quickly eliminated all unnecessary ones and shortened those that were unduly long, which forced people to maximize output per minute of meeting time. Team members also became much more selective about requests for new meetings. Although individual managers at Ford are not required to eliminate one meeting before another can be scheduled, the company's executives treat organizational time as fixed.

The centerpiece of Ford's approach is a weekly session called the Business Plan Review (BPR). It brings together the company's most senior executives in a focused four- to five-hour session to set strategy and review performance. That by itself reduced the senior team's meeting time from about fifty hours a month to about twenty. Moreover, content for the session was standardized, reducing the extensive prep time previously required. Substituting the BPR for the "meetings week" liberated thousands of hours at Ford, enabling the company to lower overhead costs at a time when rivals were seeking a government bailout. It also improved the quality and pace of decision making at the company, accelerating Ford's turnaround.

A company that can establish a fixed time budget could at some point choose to start each year with a clean slate. Just as many companies develop their operating and capital budgets from scratch each year, a company that was serious about time management might decide to examine every regularly scheduled meeting to determine whether it was really necessary.

Establish clear delegations of authority for time investments. Most companies place few restrictions on who can organize a meeting. Decisions regarding how long the session should be, who should attend, and even whether participants must attend in person are frequently left up to low-level employees. The result: costly meetings are scheduled without scrutiny.

At another manufacturing company we worked with recently, the leadership team took two simple steps to rein in unproductive meeting time. First, it reduced the default meeting length from sixty minutes to thirty. Second, it established a guideline limiting meetings to seven or fewer participants. Any meeting exceeding ninety minutes or including more than seven people had to be approved by the supervisor of the convener's supervisor (two levels up). This cut the organizational time budget dramatically—by the equivalent of two hundred full-time employees over a six-month period.

Create a new protocol for e-communications. We often tell clients and audiences that we have one simple, free piece of consulting advice for liberating unproductive time: eliminate "Reply All" on the company's system. We mean this facetiously, but there's more than a grain of truth in it. Indiscriminate copying of messages to everyone who might possibly be interested clutters up inboxes and wastes huge amounts of time. If people had to type in every recipient's name, they would be considerably more careful about which individuals they put on the "To" or "CC" lists. Emails and responses would undoubtedly decline, probably dramatically.

Many companies have found it useful to spell out rules and protocols for emails. At one large technology company, a time audit revealed that employees at all levels of the organization were spending nearly half a day each week reading and responding to emails that they should never have received in the first place. Senior leaders were aghast. As a first step, they decided to role-model new behaviors regarding email. They reduced the number of one-to-many emails they sent. They resisted responding to emails sent to them "for information only." And they started to call out others who were copying them on emails that they did not need to receive. With time, the leaders' practices caught on, and managers at other levels of the organization altered their behavior. The result: far less of the organization's time was wasted on unnecessary e-communications.

Provide real-time feedback to manage organizational load. It's said that we can't manage what we don't measure. Yet few organizations routinely track the critical variables affecting human productivity, such as meeting time, meeting attendance, and email volume. Without such monitoring, it is hard to manage those factors—or even to know the magnitude of your organization's productivity problem. And without a baseline measure of productivity, setting targets for improvement becomes impossible.

Many executives already review how much time they spend with various constituencies and on various issues, using just their own calendars. A few companies, including Seagate and Boeing, have experimented with giving their executives real-time feedback on the "load" they are putting on the organization in terms of meetings, emails, IMs, and so forth. At Seagate, some senior managers participated in a program in which they routinely received reports quantifying their individual loads along with the average load generated by other executives at their level and in their function. This information, combined with guidelines from the top, encouraged them to modify their behavior to liberate organizational time.[6]

2. Run meetings that work

And then there are meetings. No company can eliminate all of them; some meetings are essential for fostering collaboration and making critical decisions. But most companies can dramatically improve the quality of the meetings they do hold by establishing a few simple norms:

- Be sure a meeting is appropriate. Meetings are great for some tasks, like gathering input and coming to a group decision. They aren't so good for others, such as drafting a strategy document. Before calling a meeting, decide whether it's really the best way to get the job done.

- Set a clear—and selective—agenda. A surprising number of meetings don't have an agenda. One study found that 32 percent of meetings lacked an agenda, and only 29 percent of meetings had a written agenda that was distributed to all attendees in advance. A clear agenda communicates priorities. It also tells people what they can safely postpone or ignore.

- **Reduce meeting time whenever possible.** In general, people can concentrate on a single topic for an average of about eighteen minutes. Switching topics makes it possible to reengage participants, but there's a limit of about forty-five minutes in all. In conference calls, people stop paying attention after an average of twenty-three minutes.

- **Insist on advance preparation.** One study reported that as many as one-third of meeting participants do not prepare for a meeting at all. At Ford, all materials for weekly BPRs must be distributed in advance so that participants can review them ahead of time. That greatly reduces the time devoted to information sharing during the BPR. At Amazon, CEO Jeff Bezos expects carefully written reports—no PowerPoint presentations—at every meeting of top executives. Then he gives attendees thirty minutes at the start of the meeting to read these reports.

- **Practice good meeting hygiene.** Clarify the purpose of every meeting. Spell out people's roles in decisions. Create a decision log that captures every decision made in a meeting. (If the log is blank, you'll find that people begin questioning why the meeting was held at all.) Oh, yes: start on time. Beginning each hour-long meeting only five minutes late costs a company 8 percent of its meeting time. Most management teams wouldn't tolerate 8 percent waste in any other area of responsibility.

- End early, particularly if the meeting is going nowhere. If the meeting schedule calls for sixty minutes, most companies' meetings almost always last the full sixty minutes, whether they need to or not. That's crazy. At Apple, Jobs used to "call an audible" when the productivity of a meeting started to decline or participants were unprepared. Some people considered his style abrupt, but he prevented the waste of time and money in a session that was unlikely to produce the desired outcome.

Also, don't forget to manage the invite list. In many companies it's bad form not to ask lots of participants to a meeting. What people don't realize is that every additional attendee adds cost. Unnecessary attendees also get in the way. Remember the rule of seven: every attendee over seven reduces the likelihood of making a good, quick, executable decision by 10 percent. Once you hit sixteen or seventeen participants, your decision effectiveness is close to zero. The corollary of this principle is that people should decline invitations to meetings they feel they shouldn't attend. Attending a meeting ought to be a signal: "This meeting is so important that I am willing to set aside everything else that I could be doing to join with the other attendees."[7]

And if too many people show up anyway? Recently, we heard a story about a US undersecretary of defense who was managing procurement. She came to her first meeting with contractors and saw some sixty people in the room. So she said, "Let's first create a big circle. We'll go around the room, and everyone can say who they are and why they're here." Participants rolled their eyes—did they really have to do something this gimmicky?—but did as she asked. After the first two had identified themselves, the undersecretary said, "Thanks for your interest, but we won't need you here. You can excuse yourself." Others met a similar fate. By the time she got to the tenth person in the circle, people all over the room were getting up to leave, knowing they had no real reason to be there. Eventually the group got down to around twelve members—and the productivity of that meeting rose about fivefold.

3. Take a holistic approach

It's tough to implement reforms like these piecemeal, because people will tend to forget about them. That's why we often recommend a major companywide effort to change meeting practices. The Australian energy company Woodside offers an example.

Woodside is the country's largest independent oil and gas company, with a $25 billion market capitalization at this writing and about 3,500 employees. But a few years ago, the mood in the organization was one of frustration. Meetings seemed to be happening all the time; in fact, a survey revealed that staff members were spending between 25 percent and 50 percent of their time in meetings, with senior leaders at the top of that range. Reports were proliferating as well, to the point where most managers were obliged to read three or four every day. And authorizations—just getting a plane ticket, for example—seemed to take forever. For a while, the company was hamstrung. Everyone was aware of the acute organizational drag, but no one could find the time to take action.

Finally, Woodside's senior leaders decided to break the logjam. They commissioned a diagnostic test to quantify the problem and build a business case for change. The diagnostic test broke down the time spent in meetings by department, by levels of the organization, even by type of meeting. It added up the time of meeting participants to put a dollar figure on the cost. Woodside has an engineering, numbers-driven culture, and these numbers were persuasive. A pilot program, executives decided, would identify a few departments that were struggling the hardest with the time issue and would try out a variety of solutions. Those that worked would be rolled out across the organization.

The pilot project focused on three units, together accounting for about 13 percent of the target workforce. Groups brainstormed ideas, evaluating them on both ease of implementation and likely effect. Then the units began implementation. Some of the ideas were remarkably simple—programming Outlook, for instance, to schedule twenty-five-minute rather than thirty-minute meetings, thus providing people who had back-to-back sessions a few minutes to get from one conference room to another. Others required more effort, such as establishing and implementing "meeting blackout" periods each week. The company tried several other techniques as well. It created tools that calculated the cost of each meeting, based on the number of attendees and the duration. It trained everyone in meeting effectiveness, including coaching gatekeepers (such as executive assistants) in how to control the meeting scheduling process. It assessed every recurring meeting to be sure it was necessary, and it issued weekly reports for leaders showing actual meeting hours compared to personal and team targets.

The pilot project was successful, and the most effective measures were rolled out over the following nine months. The results? Time in meetings was reduced by an average of 20 percent, equating to about 5 percent of total full-time-equivalent capacity. Some 70 percent of the staff reported feeling that meeting effectiveness had improved. "I now feel more empowered to decline meeting invites where my attendance is not necessary," said one manager. Said another, "My meetings are better structured and more effective as attendees come better prepared to contribute." A third poignantly revealed just how important such a change can be:

> I must admit that I attended the introductory session . . . with skeptical reluctance. I was particularly shocked to find that I spend an average of twenty-two hours a week in meetings. However, I was not surprised, as a majority of my effective working time has been pushed to late nights and weekends. Both my team and my family were suffering the side effects of my lack of availability.
>
> I have already seen a major improvement in my work-life balance and time spent at my desk. It is the beginning of a journey to make the most of my time in the office and restore my work-life balance.

When a company stops wasting time, people feel as if a load has been lifted from their shoulders.

As Peter Drucker said, time is an organization's scarcest resource. No amount of money can buy a twenty-five-hour day or reclaim an hour squandered in an unproductive meeting. To get the most out of its workforce, an organization needs to treat time as the scarce resource that it is, creating disciplined time budgets and investing organizational time to generate the greatest possible value for the institution and its owners. Good time management is a first step toward unleashing the productive power of your organization's employees. In the following chapter, we'll delve a little deeper and figure out how you can attack the problem at its roots.

THREE WAYS TO LIBERATE YOUR
ORGANIZATION'S TIME

1. *Who knows where the time goes?* Using today's tools, a company can track all the meetings and communications that eat up so many hours. It's a great way to determine the magnitude of the problem.

2. *Time is money—and should be treated as such.* That means creating time budgets, monitoring time investments, and reducing wasted time.

3. *Meeting management is essential.* Good meeting practices can eliminate vast quantities of wasted time—and can make the meetings that remain far more productive.

3

Simplify the
Operating Model

Disciplined time management allows your organization to get more done more efficiently. There's less wheel-spinning, less yield loss, fewer wasted hours. But what if the work should never have been done in the first place? What if far fewer people could be planning, performing, and approving the necessary tasks?

At many companies, the principal source of organizational drag is the sheer complexity of the organization and the resulting bloat of business units, functions, and task forces. Sasol, the South Africa–based energy and chemicals company, recently transformed its organization to reduce drag, but before it began, it had 46 business units and functions reporting to the Group Executive Committee, 210 subsidiary companies, 72 legal entities (in South Africa alone), and 49 separate corporate committees. In such a situation, it's hard for anyone to know who's doing what, who's responsible for what, and whether people are working in an optimal way to add value for customers. Productivity suffers accordingly.

But Sasol is hardly alone. Complexity and bloat of this sort crop up throughout the corporate world. You may recognize the symptoms in your own organization:

- Slow decisions. Every major decision seems to involve numerous stakeholders, and they all must have their say. So decisions take forever. At another large natural-resources company, hiring a new general manager for a mine required the involvement of three human resources professionals, four regional leaders, and two executives from corporate. Getting all these people to agree on a new hire typically took months. In the meantime, positions sat open and promising candidates were snapped up by faster-moving competitors.

- A culture of "swirl." People review data that no one cares about. They write reports that no one reads. They prepare presentations that never lead to a decision. Before long, a culture of "swirl" develops, in which every new issue generates additional work and cost without producing results. If you were to draw this toxic culture on paper, it would look something like the swirl in figure 3-1.

- Administrative costs out of control. General and administrative expense as a percentage of sales creeps upward. The increase is concentrated in management and support functions. Sasol found that its cash fixed costs had risen an average of four percentage points a year more than inflation from 2007 to 2012, even though production was essentially flat. The ranks of management had swelled about twice as much as overall head-count growth.

FIGURE 3-1

A culture of swirl

Complex organizations are often paralyzed by bureaucratic "swirl" and lose focus on what matters.

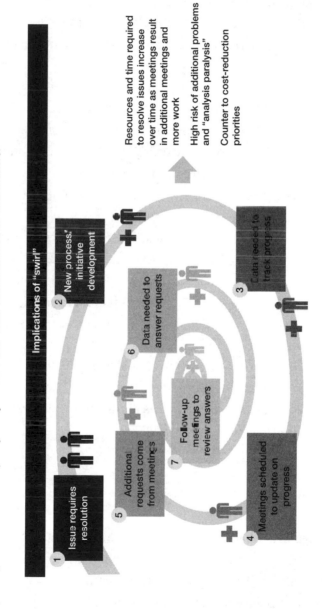

Implications of "swirl"

Resources and time required to resolve issues increase over time as meetings result in additional meetings and more work

High risk of additional problems and "analysis paralysis"

Counter to cost-reduction priorities

1 Issue requires resolution

2 New process, initiative development

3 Data needed to track progress

4 Meetings scheduled to update on progress

5 Additional requests come from meetings

6 Data needed to answer requests

7 Follow-up meetings to review answers

Source: Bain Brief, "Four Paths to a Focused Organization"

Many companies have time-honored methods of attacking this kind of cost creep and organizational bloat. First, they issue a directive: no merit increases this year. Next comes the hiring freeze. Then there's a change in the 401(k) match or other benefit reductions. Finally, management issues a mandate to cut staff across the board. If all these measures don't achieve the desired effects—and they rarely do—the executive team decides to mount a comprehensive cost-reduction effort, often including restructuring the organization. Yet the organizational drag doesn't go away. "We have a cost containment project or restructuring every couple of years," complained the managing director of a Sasol business unit. "But we're not learning from our experiences."

Drag doesn't go away because this approach is misguided. If you take out people but don't take out the *work*, the people inevitably creep back in. Likewise, if you take out work but don't take out people, the work will come back, too. The real source of organizational drag is unnecessary tasks, murky accountabilities, and the complexity that produces them. So you have to tackle organizational complexity at its root in order to unleash productive power.

Let's look at the dimensions of this problem, and at what to do about each one.

Revenge of the nodes

Organizational complexity is often misunderstood. It's viewed as a temporary affliction, something that infects an organization like an illness. In reality it is a natural outcome of growth. As companies expand, they inevitably add product lines and business units. They open up new channels, geographic regions, and customer segments. They merge and acquire. Each of these moves creates a new organizational element, and every new element has to intersect and interact with every other element. These intersections—we call them *nodes*—are the fundamental source of complexity in most companies.

To see why this is so, imagine a simple business with two product lines and five functions. Every time leaders make a decision spanning products and functions, it requires eleven interactions—one between each of the two product organizations and each of the five functions, and one between the product organizations themselves. Now imagine that the company wants to get closer to the customer and adds just two customer units to its organization. The number of interactions for cross-business decisions doesn't rise by just two, from eleven to thirteen; instead it rises by fifteen, from eleven to twenty-six (see figure 3-2). Organizational complexity more than doubles, fed by a geometric increase in the number of nodes.[1]

This isn't a theoretical issue—it's a real one. At the University of California, Berkeley, every academic department had its own HR, IT, finance, and administrative staff, creating countless nodes for major administrative decisions. A major energy company found itself in a similar predicament: it had created many general managers over the years in hopes of encouraging executives to think like owners—and each of these new GMs expected to have his or her own HR staff, IT department, finance department, quality department, and so on. In this case, the number of nodes had skyrocketed from eight hundred to twelve thousand over a ten-year period.

Each node that is added can (and usually does) lead to more interactions. Some of these interactions are valuable, of course. But others are less so: their purpose may be no more

FIGURE 3-2

Nodes increase geometrically

A simple product function matrix has only 11 "nodes" of interaction, but adding just 2 units on a third dimension creates 26 nodes—more than double the complexity.

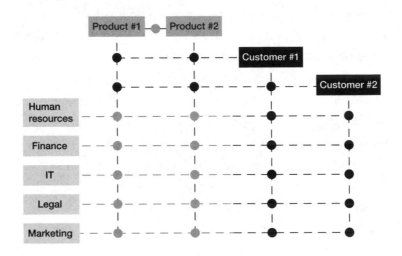

Source: Bain & Company

than to agree on data, to manage new stakeholders, or to prepare for the next meeting. As the number of nodes proliferates, so does the number of interactions it takes to get work done. In a 2015 study, the research and advisory firm CEB found that more than 60 percent of employees now must interact with ten or more people every day to do their job; 30 percent must interact with twenty or more. These percentages have increased consistently over the last five years. CEB also found that between 35 percent and 40 percent of managers "are so overloaded [by collaboration] that it's actually impossible for them to get work done effectively," according to researcher Brian Kropp.[2]

To assess the spread of complexity in your own company, create a "nodal map" of the organization's critical decisions. Take a limited set of cross-company decisions—say, mergers and acquisitions, new product launches, new market entry, large capital programs, and the like. These should be decisions that have a big impact on the company's value and are made periodically. Now describe the number of organizations that need to be involved in making these decisions (for example, manufacturing, marketing, finance, and human resources); how they are involved (generating data, reviewing analysis); and how they interact (such as through committees or governance meetings). Carefully map the precise number of interactions or decision nodes required to make and execute just one significant decision.

The findings from this simple exercise can be eye-opening. At one large company, the advertising group had to run every proposed campaign through all of the company's business units, its product groups, and the corporate marketing group, perhaps ten nodes in all. If a campaign encountered any kind of objection during this approval process—a common event in advertising— team members would have to go back through all the nodes again. So the number of possible interactions was far greater even than the number of nodes. At another company, leaders examined the number of reports created to support major R&D investments. They found that each function, business, and customer group created its own presentation to advocate for its own pet projects. Each of these reports required hours to gather the necessary information and analyze it. Lengthy appendixes accompanied most of the presentations. Yet senior leaders never reviewed the vast majority—more than 60 percent.

In our experience, mapping nodal complexity for a select number of critical decisions creates a burning platform, a sense of urgency about the need for change. Once leaders see the complexity involved in making and executing critical decisions, most want to take immediate action to simplify the organization.

Spans and layers: never the whole solution

Faced with growing complexity, many companies rely on a time-honored fix: call in the consultants to study the number of managerial layers in the organization and each manager's span of control. The point, usually, is to assess whether the organization would work better (or at least as well) with broader spans of control and fewer managerial layers. If it could, it would have fewer supervisors and, thus, lower costs. Companies often apply rough benchmarks, such as the "rule of eight"—meaning that no manager should have fewer than eight direct reports. Then they restructure everything that doesn't fit these benchmarks.[3]

The logic behind a spans-and-layers approach is powerful: unnecessary supervisors do create work and don't increase efficiency, thus lowering an organization's productivity. Indeed, companies often underestimate how expensive all those supervisors really are. Not long ago, we studied the cost of adding a manager or executive and found a kind of multiplier effect. When you hire a manager, he or she typically generates enough work to keep somebody else busy as well. Senior executives— senior vice presidents and executive vice presidents—are even more costly. These high-priced folks typically require support from a caravan of assistants and chiefs of staff. This support staff generates a lot more work for other people, too. The extra burden comes to 4.2 full-time equivalents per hire, including the executive's own time (see figure 3-3).[4]

So spans-and-layers changes that eliminate unnecessary supervisors can be helpful. But they're helpful only if they are done right. The rule of eight, for instance, is rarely applicable. Highly repetitive transactional work can typically support a broad span of control, involving perhaps fifteen or more people under one supervisor. Specialized work requires closer

FIGURE 3-3

The true cost of your next manager

As managers move up the hierarchy, their need for support staff grows. Here's how much time this takes up for everyone involved.

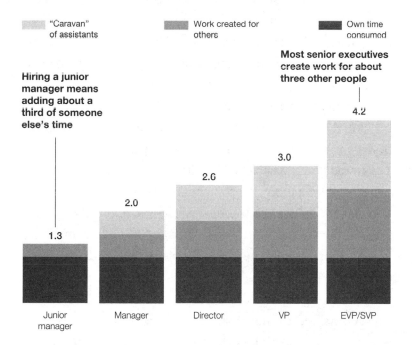

Source: Michael C. Mankins, "The True Cost of Hiring Yet Another Manager," *Harvard Business Review,* June 2014.

supervision and thus a narrower span, often fewer than five. The task is not simply to delayer but to tailor the supervisory structure to the job at hand.

It's also important to identify issues that don't show up in most spans-and-layers analyses. A large defense contractor, for instance, was facing close scrutiny of its defense program, with the government strongly pressuring the company to reduce costs. Analysis showed that the company had a reasonable number of layers and that its spans of control were actually broader than benchmarks. A closer look, however, revealed that, while many managers had a significant number of direct reports—some as many as fourteen—only one or two of those direct reports were "line" managers who had others working under them. The others (up to twelve each) were "staff" who helped prepare documentation, focused on processes and approvals, and so on. While these huge staffs worked on issues in the background, other big groups were tasked with trying to get today's work out today. As an example, a single complex engineering change involved 125 people and more than 700 interactions. No wonder things were bogging down, yet everyone believed that they were doing the best they could to ensure a quality product, and that the organization was "lean," relative to benchmarks.

The real limitation of spans-and-layers changes, however, is that they don't address the root cause of complexity. If there are too many nodes, decisions will always be slow and costs will continue to creep upward. If a piece of work doesn't need to be done, it makes no difference whether it is done in a unit with an average span of two, six, or twenty-six. Eliminating supervisors and changing the span of control doesn't get rid of that work. And unless the work is taken out, the people required to do it—and the corresponding costs—will shortly reappear.

So the essential task—one that stymies too many companies—is to eliminate unnecessary nodes and unnecessary work. Here's how to go about it.

Clarify your operating model

Every big company has an operating model, either explicit or implicit. The operating model is the link between strategy and execution. It outlines the company's high-level structure—by product line, by geographical region or country, by function, by customer, and so on. It defines decision rights and accountabilities. It also serves as a blueprint for how the company will organize resources to accomplish its critical tasks. The model thus encompasses a host of essential decisions, including:

- What the shape and size of each business will be

- Where the boundaries are between each line of business

- How people work together within and across these boundaries

- How the corporate center will add value to the business units

- What norms and behaviors the company wants to encourage

The number and types of people you need, and the organizational shape those people work in (as depicted by spans and layers), are *outputs*; they reflect your choices of operating model.

The graphic in figure 3-4 lays out the simplified elements of an operating model and explains how each contributes to the work completed in an organization. *Structure* determines

FIGURE 3-4

Simplify the operating model to eliminate work

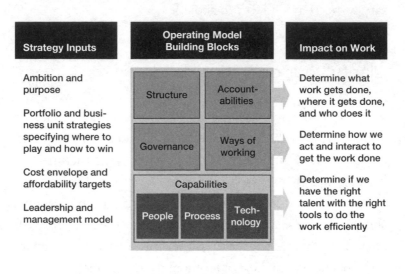

Strategy Inputs	Operating Model Building Blocks		Impact on Work
Ambition and purpose	Structure	Account-abilities	Determine what work gets done, where it gets done, and who does it
Portfolio and business unit strategies specifying where to play and how to win	Governance	Ways of working	Determine how we act and interact to get the work done
Cost envelope and affordability targets	Capabilities		Determine if we have the right talent with the right tools to do the work efficiently
Leadership and management model	People	Process	Technology	

Source: Bain & Company

the potential number of nodes. *Accountabilities* determine which nodes are activated or deactivated through assignment of responsibility, authority, and resourcing. *Governance* determines the frequency and nature of interactions across nodes. And *ways of working* shape how efficiently and effectively people execute these interactions. To take work out of an organization—and to make it stay out—a company must systematically address each element of the operating model.[5]

1. Simplify the structure

A complex operating model invariably leads to a complex structure and too many decision nodes. Yet that's the trap many big companies are caught in: their operating models are needlessly complex. Rather than choose a dominant dimension for decision making, for example, they adopt a variety of overlapping structures or intricate matrix organizations with different (and potentially conflicting) dotted-line accountabilities. Holding your company's operating model up to the light offers the opportunity both to simplify it and to make sure that it reflects your company's strategy.

That's essentially what Sasol did. The largest energy and chemical company in South Africa, it was prestigious, prosperous, and financially successful. But the company's leaders had two critical concerns. One was the steady increase in cash fixed costs that we mentioned earlier, well above the rate of inflation. The second was the company's remarkable level of organizational complexity, with all those business units, functions, and committees. Both of these concerns had been masked by oil prices, but the company would be vulnerable if prices declined. "We had created multiple BUs over the years to drive growth," explained one executive. But, "while we had been very successful in growing the business, this had also created multiple silos in the organization; we were very much busy doing business with ourselves rather than being fully focused on the market and sustained profitability." Many Sasol managers, for example, felt they were spending far too much time in meetings discussing issues such as transfer pricing and interface complexities. Moreover, getting a decision on major issues could take weeks, because the decisions were tied up in one or another committee. If the market environment suddenly changed, executives worried, how quickly would Sasol be able to respond?

So Sasol rebuilt its operating model to focus on each part of the value chain—buy, make, and sell—grouping its businesses into upstream, operations, and sales and marketing divisions. It created one overall profit-and-loss statement, with activities grouped to optimize company margins. It reduced the number of business units and functions by more than one-third, so that it was spending less time "doing business with ourselves." It cut the number of South African legal entities through which it conducted its business from 72 to 35, with further plans to reduce to below 20 entities. (That move alone significantly reduced the workload for the company's finance, legal, and administrative functions.) And it streamlined its corporate committees, reducing the number of committees from 49 to 13 and lowering the number of participants in each one. Complementing these structural moves was a concentrated focus on just three essential behaviors: buying into a common game plan, trusting everyone to deliver on agreed-on accountabilities, and acting in the best interests of the Sasol Group rather than one's own unit. The company's top managers signed a document pledging to live up to these standards—a symbolic act that reflected the CEO's commitment cascading throughout the organization.

The effects were felt up and down the company. "The impact [of these moves] on leadership was tremendous," said one executive. Many hours were saved: "We are spending 60 percent-plus less time in internal and governance meetings than we used to, and we are able to use the freed-up time to focus on managing the business." Decisions are made quicker: when oil prices dropped, Sasol was the first in its industry to go to market with a comprehensive response plan. And the company is far more efficient than before: the growth rate of cash fixed costs dropped from four percentage points above inflation to eight points below.[6]

2. Zero-base the nodes

But even companies with a robust structure can find themselves performing redundant or unnecessary work. One company might have businesses organized around both products and countries. Each of these units will feel responsible for sales; each will compile its own data; and each will launch its own initiatives, not necessarily coordinated with one another. Another company might have a global finance function supplemented by regional finance offices. Chances are that both will compile similar reports, and that the information in one won't necessarily match information in the other.

It's helpful in this context to zero-base the nodes, much as you would zero-base a budget. If you were creating the organization from scratch, what would it look like? Which nodes are essential, and which could you eliminate? We have a simple axiom for simplifying an organization's nodal structure.

Do less, do it better, do it only once, and do it in the right place. If you have a global finance organization, for instance, it's unlikely that you'll need both a regional finance organization and country-by-country finance organizations. To be sure, there may be good reasons for occasional duplication. You may need to structure a compliance function by country to take legal differences into account while a global compliance office ensures that multinational operations stay within worldwide guidelines. But the point is to reduce duplication wherever possible.

A node usually involves a manager (though not every manager represents a node) and a set of decision rights. Decision rights need to be spelled out, as we discuss later in the chapter. But not all nodes are created equal. The intersection of a large product or service line with a major geographical region is likely to involve a lot of revenue. A senior executive who is accountable for major decisions and who likely has P&L responsibility will manage it. By contrast, the intersection of a regional business unit with a smaller geographic area (such as a country) will probably involve only a junior manager with limited decision rights and no P&L. "Heavier" nodes—those that involve more work and greater complexity—should be addressed first. And business value, such as the amount of revenue involved, should be a key factor in deciding where to keep, add, or eliminate nodes.

A tech company we worked with recently is a case in point. Before our work, the organization was structured along a three-dimensional matrix—geography, industry vertical, and product or service line. Each of these three dimensions had a P&L, and all the P&L leaders believed that they should control all of the resources required to manage the performance of their particular unit. In effect, every node in the company's three-dimensional matrix was treated as if it had equal weight, and each interacted with HR, finance, IT, and other support functions. After careful consideration, the company's leaders determined that the geographic dimension of the matrix was most essential to executing the company's strategy. From then on, geographic leaders were held accountable for profit and loss, service lines were responsible for costs and quality, and industries were reframed as centers of excellence, with no P&L accountability and minimal investment authority. By zero-basing the nodes required to execute the company's strategy, the business reduced the number of nodes by more than 25 percent. This node reduction has paved the way for increased productivity.

3. Deactivate nodes when they are no longer adding value

Companies know how to *do* things. They innovate, expand, launch initiatives, and, of course, they add nodes. They have elaborate processes for all these moves; every January, they create the "to do" priorities for the year. What they don't usually know is how to *stop* doing things. There are few if any processes for killing unsuccessful initiatives and eliminating unnecessary parts of the organization. Perhaps a company creates "centers of excellence," for example. Later, if the centers have turned out to be dysfunctional or just superfluous, they nevertheless live on because there is no process for terminating them. For example, one utility we worked with some time ago had spent several years overhauling its enterprise resource planning (ERP) system. Twelve months after completion of the project, the steering committee still met for two hours a week to "review progress." Not surprisingly, there was very little progress to review, but the meeting still consumed valuable time. Except in a crisis, companies rarely have a list of "stop" priorities. One of the most powerful steps any executive can take is to simply say, "Stop!"

In addition to ending unnecessary initiatives—particularly those that are complete—there are two other cease-and-desist orders that can be valuable. One is to eliminate multiple sources of data. Whenever different units of a company generate reports, the chances are good that the reports won't wholly agree with one another, and that someone will therefore be given the job of reconciling them. A company can avoid that unnecessary work by establishing a "single source of truth" for all its decisions. The other is to determine which functions are essential to your strategy and invest disproportionately in those, rather than spreading investment dollars across the board. "Leadership set the tone in focusing activity on what adds value for the business," says a Sasol executive. "An adjective we started to use very often was 'fit for purpose' instead of trying to be 'world class' or 'best practice' everywhere."

4. Minimize the number of interactions between the nodes

Nodes are just people, and the more people you have to inter-act with, the more time you are likely to spend in unnecessary interactions. Aligning the structures of different groups en-ables you to reduce and simplify the interactions required to perform key functions. Dell offers a great example. Like many technology companies, Dell has multiple parties involved in selling its products to commercial customers. An account ex-ecutive manages the relationship with each customer. Once a specific product need is identified, he or she will call on prod-uct specialists and engineers to tailor Dell's offer to best meet the customer's need. Historically, Dell organized its account executives by industry vertical—health care, web tech, and so on. But the company's product specialists and engineers were organized by product and then by geographic region, not by vertical. To make sales of the same product solution to the same type of customer (say, a health-care organization), an individual account executive would have to work with one group of specialists in the Northwest, another group in the Southwest, and so on—many different interactions to make the same kind of sale.

So Dell took measures to reduce the number of interactions. It aligned the structure of its account executives with that of its product specialists and engineers by shifting its account ex-ecutive organization to a geographic structure. As a result, the number of product specialists and engineers an individual ac-count executive needed to interact with was reduced substan-tially, from eleven individuals to an average of five. That meant less wasted time learning how to work with a new group of people and higher levels of sales productivity.

A second way of simplifying the nodal structure is to spell out decision rights so that they are crystal clear. Much interaction between nodes, after all, is politicking. People want to protect their turf. They want a voice in decisions. When decision rights are spelled out and agreed on, much of that back-and-forthing disappears. So the tasks here are to unpack the process of making and executing key decisions, and then to ensure that everyone understands his or her role.

Bain has a decision-rights tool called RAPID that can help; it's a loose acronym for the five key roles in preparing for a decision, making it, and then seeing it through to action:

- R is for *recommend*. The individual or team that "has the R" is responsible for gathering data, assessing alternative courses of action, and coming up with a recommendation.

- I is for *input*. The "R" team consults with people who have relevant expertise, asking for their input. The "I" folks do not have a veto, and they do not have responsibility for the recommendation.

- A is for *agree*. People with "A" responsibilities—often in legal or compliance—must sign off on the alternatives that are being considered before they are evaluated and a recommendation is presented to the decision maker.

- D is for *decide*. At most companies, for most critical decisions, one individual should "have the D" and take responsibility for the decision.

- P is for *perform*. The team with "P" responsibilities has the job of executing the decision in a timely fashion.[7]

Companies typically go through a full RAPID exercise—assigning explicit decision roles—only for critical decisions, those that carry a lot of value. Of course, the "critical decision" category is broader than sometimes imagined. It includes not only big, one-off decisions like major capital investments but also day-to-day decisions that add up to a lot of value over time. But veteran RAPID users find that there's a spillover effect as well. Once accustomed to defining decision rights for major decisions, managers tend to use the thinking and the language in their everyday jobs ("You have the D for this one, Bob"). The tool thus helps clarify decision roles throughout the organization.

Woodside, the Australian oil and gas company, is again illustrative. The company had been operating with a matrix structure for many years. Although the matrix was designed to foster greater collaboration across the company, decision authority and accountability were murky. As a result, the time spent coordinating across functions and business units increased dramatically, adding costs. In 2012, Woodside's leadership explicitly defined a set of operating principles that spelled out responsibilities, authority, and accountability for the business units, the functions, and the corporate center. A broad training program helped ensure that the company's top leaders understood the new principles and the implications for their units. A small network of navigators was established to help remove roadblocks and accelerate decision making across the company.

The impact of these changes has been profound. Given clarity on who is accountable for important decisions, executives at Woodside have streamlined how those decisions are made, liberating time. A significant portion of that time is now spent in efforts to improve execution and identify new growth opportunities for the company.

Well-defined decision roles help keep the complexity out. That's important, because nodes have a way of reinserting themselves into a company's operations. There's no mystery about this: the vice president for product engineering feels he should have a say in how the product is marketed, and the vice president of marketing feels she needs to be consulted about which features are to be included in the latest model. These nodal interactions can lead to contention unless the roles are clear.

5. Shrink the pyramid, don't just flatten it

We return now to spans and layers, which are still an essential element of an organization's structure and may need to be addressed. A company that has simplified its nodal complexity has opportunities that weren't there before. It can actually shrink the organizational pyramid rather than just flattening it by broadening spans and eliminating layers.

Shrinking the pyramid starts from a couple of simple observations. One is that an organization with a span of eight isn't any better than an organization with a span of two if the organization shouldn't exist at all. The real challenge isn't to restructure existing units; it's to identify the minimum number of units required to accomplish the essential work of the company. A second observation is that many companies, like the defense contractor mentioned earlier, have a disproportionate number of "watchers" as opposed to "doers." Executives are some distance away from front-line responsibilities. They tend to bring their posses of watchers to meetings so that the whole team can be fully informed, produce whatever data the meeting requires, and follow up on any loose ends afterward.

A company that sets out to shrink the pyramid goes about things with a different mindset. It essentially starts with a clean sheet for the entire structure, determining the minimum number of people required to make and execute the necessary decisions. It assumes that managers will be player-coaches, actively involved in getting work done, rather than distant bosses. It eliminates people whose only value is reviewing and approving—in effect, taking out much of that kind of work. The effect of this approach is to greatly reduce the number of managerial layers. And even though it may actually decrease the average span of control, it makes for much more efficient and effective operation.

There's no pat formula about what the organization should look like because companies participate in industries with substantially different competitive dynamics. Anheuser-Busch InBev (AB InBev) operates in a relatively mature category where cost management is key to value creation and competitive success. It operates with several fewer layers than most companies and with modest spans of control, thus ensuring that everyone is a doer and no one is a bureaucratic manager. As a result, the overall organization is remarkably lean. The company says to its managers, in effect, you are responsible for these people but you won't have time to micromanage them because you will have a lot on your own plate. Google, which operates in a rapidly growing and dynamic marketplace, has a different organizational model but achieves a similar outcome in terms of how managers interact with teams. At Google, most work is done by autonomous teams, and each manager has a very broad span of control. Google says to its managers, in effect, your job is not to supervise the individuals who are nominally reporting to you; your job is to help the teams succeed. You will have too many direct reports to micromanage them. Both models start with a clean sheet, resulting in a structure that is no larger than it needs to be to execute each company's strategy efficiently and effectively.

————————

Organizational drag is a crippling illness. The company suffering from it wastes time, performs unnecessary tasks, and operates inefficiently. Curing the organization of this illness requires the kind of careful, sustained time management and complexity-reduction measures that we have described here and in the previous chapter. But creating a true high-performance organization involves much more than merely getting rid of drag. It means attracting, cultivating, and deploying great talent. It means engaging and inspiring people so that the organization can draw on their enthusiasm and creativity. And it means building a culture in which employees see the organization as theirs—as something they care about and want to help succeed. We now turn to these tasks in part two.

THREE WAYS TO SIMPLIFY YOUR OPERATING MODEL

1. *Count up the nodes.* Executives often find themselves surprised by the number of nodes, or intersections, in their organizations. That's why big decisions take so much time; each one has to wend its way through many nodes.

2. *Hold your operating model up to the light.* Look at structure, accountabilities, governance, and ways of working.

Nearly every company can simplify its operating model on each of these dimensions.

3. *Think about spans and layers in this context.* Conventional spans-and-layers analyses often don't accomplish much, because spans and layers are really an output of your operating model.

PART TWO

TALENT

People are not your most important
asset. The right people are.

—Jim Collins

A company that follows the prescriptions in part one will reduce organizational drag. It will save some of its people's precious time and thereby help them become more productive. But it will not yet be reaching anything like its full potential. The best companies, as we see in our research, gain a whopping twenty-nine points on the productive power index just by attracting, retaining, and above all deploying great people in ways that maximize their output. The other three quartiles, unfortunately, gain only four points from managing their talent effectively.

So talent matters. But not just any talent. What really makes the difference is people who bring a unique set of skills and experiences to the workplace, and who can learn to work together in teams on the initiatives that are critical to your company's success. Chapter 4 focuses on these A-level players, the ones who truly make a difference. It discusses how many you are likely to need (not everyone is an A-level player, after all) and what roles to put them in. It will help you find, evaluate, develop them over time, and deploy them where they can have the biggest impact. Knowing who these difference makers are is a job for the CEO, because there are fewer in most large companies than you might think.

Chapter 5 looks at talent from another angle. Steve Jobs probably said it best: "Great things in business are never done by one person, they're done by a team of people." But how much attention does the typical company pay to assembling and managing its teams? In our experience, far too little. Executives are likely to make up a team from whoever happens to be available and then wonder why it doesn't accomplish much. The best performers, by contrast, take a far more disciplined approach to teaming. These companies form all-star teams, as we'll describe in this chapter. If you need to get something done, done quickly, and done right, the chances are you will need a team of A-level players.

Here, too, we'll have some stories to tell and some controversies to stir up. We'll offer several telling examples to illustrate how much better "the best" really are. We'll show why the conventional nine-box assessment of managers' performance and potential is close to useless. We'll show why NASCAR driver Kyle Busch can win so many races, how Boeing filled a critical gap in its product lineup faster than ever before, and how Ford and Dell turned themselves around partly by paying attention to teaming.

Pretty much every company knows it should have as many great people as it can find. But if all that talent isn't to wither on the vine—if those great people instead continue to develop, to make an impact, and to work productively with other great people—they have to be managed as the scarce resource they are. *That's* where you make a difference.

4

Find and Develop the "Difference Makers"

Everyone knows that great people—A-level talent—can make a difference to an organization's performance. Not everyone understands just how much of a difference they make. Consider a few examples:

- The best fish butcher at Le Bernardin restaurant in New York can portion as much fish in an hour as the average prep cook can manage in three hours.

- The best developer at Apple writes nine times more usable code per day than the average software engineer in Silicon Valley.

- The best blackjack dealer at Caesars Palace in Las Vegas keeps his table playing at least five times as long as the average dealer on the Strip.

- The best sales associate at Nordstrom sells at least eight times as much as the average sales associate walking the floor at other department stores.

- The best transplant surgeon at Cleveland Clinic has a patient-survival rate at least six times longer than that of the average transplant surgeon.

Of course, there may be factors other than raw ability that help to explain these gaps. But talent alone makes a huge difference. Before he became chief justice of the US Supreme Court, John Roberts prevailed in twenty-five of the thirty-nine cases he argued before the Court. That "wins" record is more than six times better than the average record of other winning attorneys (other than solicitors general) who have argued before the Court since 1950.[1]

The size of the gap between the best and the rest depends on the nature of the job (see figure 4-1). In transactional and repetitive tasks, a multiple of between three and five is common. Container Store founder Kip Tindell, for example, believes that a star performer in his business is about three times as productive as an average employee.[2] In tasks requiring more creative thinking and specialized skills, the gap may be orders of magnitude larger. Executives at Google, maybe indulging in a little hyperbole, estimate that their best engineers are three hundred times as valuable as the average. Steve Jobs once said, "I noticed that the dynamic range between what an average person could accomplish and what the best person could accomplish was 50 or 100 to 1."[3] Whatever the difference, it's significant nearly everywhere. In the Bain–Economist Intelligence Unit study, we asked respondents to estimate the average productivity increase they get from top talent—the very best in an industry or field, not just in their own company—as

FIGURE 4-1

All talent is not created equal

"The best" are often a lot better than "the rest"

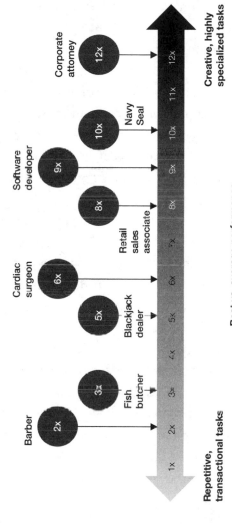

Source: Bain & Company

compared to average talent. Respondents said that the best would be, on average, 50 percent more productive than the average employee in their own company.

No company, however, wants some abstract "best." It doesn't do any good to hire the best fish butcher in the world if your business is package delivery. What you want are people who can contribute to realizing your organization's mission and delivering on its strategy better than anyone else. You want a particular kind of top talent: people who can make a difference in *your* company. And you want those difference makers in jobs where they can have the greatest impact.

That sounds like a simple goal, and it would be hard to find a CEO or chief human resources officer who would disagree with it. Unfortunately, the conventional people-management toolkit has proven time and again not to be up to the task in modern organizations. Hiring techniques, organizational hierarchies, job assignment philosophies, performance management systems, and leadership development and coaching programs all conspire to make it hard to find, develop, and deploy top talent effectively. When we asked senior leaders to estimate the percentage of their workforce that they would classify as top performers or A-level talent, the average response was slightly less than 15 percent. And that's despite the fact that most companies have spent vast sums of money in the so-called war for talent. For years, they have chased the best people, promised them fancy titles, and offered them big pay packages, yet they have little to show for it.

The outliers—those companies that seem to have cracked the code of organizational productivity—go about things differently, both philosophically and practically, and this chapter will explain some of their lessons. It will help you identify the top talent you need, the difference makers who are right for your company. It will give you fresh ideas on how to track down and evaluate difference-making talent using more advanced techniques for measuring potential. It will help you to develop these individuals through better evaluation and coaching systems, and to ensure that they are in the right jobs for the right amount of time.

Does this sound like too much nitty-gritty detail? Chances are you already manage your financial capital every bit as carefully, paying close attention to every significant investment you make. It's worth paying equal attention to your human capital, because that is what makes the real difference to a company's performance in today's world. Three critical steps can have an enormous effect on the impact of talent on workforce productivity and competitive performance.

1. Determine where your difference makers can make the biggest difference

Sounds obvious, doesn't it? But many companies somehow overlook this basic point. Following conventional practice, they continue to build their overhead budgets—the source of most expenditure on white-collar talent—using last year's as a starting point. They allocate budget increases democratically, treating each area of the business as more or less equal. They seek "functional excellence" regardless of how important a given function is to a company's mission or strategy. As a result, they end up gold-plating areas where good-enough capabilities would do just fine, and they underinvest in capabilities that are critical to their business model. Ask yourself: do our investments in human capital reflect our strategy? When we pose that question to CEOs, the answer, too often, is "I'm not sure."

So let's begin at the beginning. A robust human capital plan starts with a sharp definition of the capabilities and talent you need to build competitive advantage, given your company's strategy and business model. The process examines three issues:

- **What drives value.** What are our current and future sources of sustainable, profitable growth?

- **What capabilities are most critical.** Which capabilities and assets are essential to providing customers with products, services, and experiences different from—and better than—those provided by competitors? For these critical capabilities, where do we have gaps? Where will we gain further competitive advantage from improvement?

- **Where we should double down.** Are we sufficiently skewing our investment of scarce resources toward these critical capabilities and away from others, so that we can effectively fund our priorities?

When analyzing your capabilities, it's essential to define and assess them at a granular level. You don't have a robust capability unless it meets some key conditions. One, it should be predicated on a clear linkage to value. Two, it must be able to be delivered in a repeatable, high-quality manner with the appropriate people, processes, and technologies. Three, the company's structure, accountabilities, decision-making processes, and ways of working must support effective execution of the capability. You can then map your operating expense budgets to this capability map, comparing the funds you are investing to your strategic ambitions and requirements to test for alignment or disconnects.

Placing difference makers in business-critical roles

Armed with an understanding of where your company needs differentiated capabilities, you can determine the roles within each capability that are critical to its success. These are the roles where you want your difference makers.

Many companies' HR planning breaks down at this point. Leaders understand that no organization is made up entirely of A-level talent. They also understand that they must struggle to attract and pay for the A-level talent they require. And so they build elaborate systems for identifying, recruiting, developing, and placing these hard-to-find individuals. Where the systems go wrong, however, is that they fail to begin with the simple question: *Given our strategy and our business model, where is it critical to have A-level players shape the outcomes of our business—and where, conversely, can we live with B-level players who are capable but more easily replaceable?* They never ask themselves, in effect, "If I put an average person in this role, will it have a material impact on performance?" Putting an A-level player in a role where a B-level player will do well is a poor use of an incredibly scarce resource. And given that most executives believe they have no more than 15 percent A-level players, misplacing even a few of those individuals will significantly affect the company's productive power.

Our research and experience support the power of this intentionally inegalitarian approach. The gap between the mix of A-level talent in the best-performing companies and the rest is not significant—16 percent versus 14 percent. What's different is the way this talent is deployed (see figure 4-2). Most companies might be described as unintentionally egalitarian in their deployment of top talent. All roles, more or less, are made up of 14 percent A-level talent. The best companies, by

FIGURE 4-2

While the best and the rest have similar amounts of A-level talent, top companies focus that talent on business-critical roles

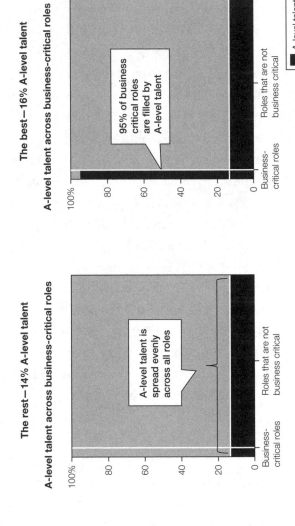

Source: Bain/EIU research (N=308)

contrast, are intentionally inegalitarian in their deployment of scarce talent. For the few roles that are business critical (say 5 percent of the total), leaders ensure that great people are in those jobs. If 95 percent or more of these roles are held by A-level talent—difference makers—then less than 12 percent of the remaining roles are held by A-level talent.

What are the business-critical roles? They do not necessarily correspond to an organization's hierarchy. Nor are they usually apparent to anyone outside the company. Rather, identifying the roles typically requires assessments such as the following:

> What are our key assets, and what do they require? In many cases, a company's key assets—proprietary intellectual property, leading brands, low-cost production assets, unique routes to market, and the like—can influence where you need A-level talent. On the one hand, you want to make sure that these assets are both protected and fully utilized. On the other, an asset or a deep capability can sometimes create enough advantage that outcomes are likely to be more or less the same, regardless of who is sitting in the decision-making chair. In the latter case, the outcomes that a B-level player generates will not be materially different from the outcomes generated by an A-level player.

> Where are our expert systems and processes insufficiently developed? Expert systems often cannot replicate the decision-making skills of a talented individual. The external environment may be so dynamic that the relevant knowledge can't be captured for a long enough period of time. Or the decision maker may sit at the intersection of a complex process that cuts across functional boundaries,

and an expert system would likely make too many costly mistakes. Consider the individuals involved in innovation, sales and operations planning, pricing, or long-term capacity planning in consumer packaged goods companies. The decisions they make can have a material impact on the company's performance precisely because they require integrated expertise that cuts across sales, marketing, R&D, and operations. A-level talent in these roles can make a big difference to bottom-line results.

Where are our skills requirements changing as our industry and business model evolve? Many consumer-facing companies have plunged headlong into Big Data, advanced analytics, and all the digital tools that accompany them. This has had a dramatic effect on key marketing and merchandising roles. Positions and professions that were once more art than science are now more science than art. The roles of the chief merchant or chief digital officer—and the types of skills required in these roles—have changed accordingly.

Why—and where—the CEO has to be involved

Despite all the calls on a CEO's time, he or she has to get involved in identifying, developing, and placing top talent. While CEOs and their chief human resource officers need a talent strategy for the entire organization, the CEO must differentially focus on the business-critical roles and the difference-making individuals who will fill them. In our experience, this will be between 100 and 150 people.

How did we reach this number? Take a company where the CEO has eight direct reports. If each direct report also has a span of control of eight, and so on, throughout the organization's layers, by the time you reach three levels below the CEO, you have roughly six hundred employees. Though every individual may be important, not all of them are going to be difference makers. In fact, it's likely that only two or three of the CEO's direct reports are themselves difference makers. If that's true in each layer and branch of the organization, then there are about 150 difference makers in the top three layers of the organization.

Interestingly, this number corresponds with Dunbar's number, described by the British anthropologist Robin Dunbar.[4] Based on his study of primates and primitive human organizations, Dunbar argues that humans can comfortably maintain only about 150 stable relationships. The premise seems to hold true in both ancient and modern forms of human organizations, including neolithic farming villages, army units in Roman times, and academic organizations within universities. Dunbar's number applies to groups that are highly motivated to work together (typically for survival), and that work or live in close proximity to one another—all conditions that appear to apply to the leadership teams of modern corporations.

So ask yourself: Can you list the 100 to 150 most critical positions in your organization, given your business model, strategy, assets, and capabilities? Who are the 100 to 150 difference makers in your company? Are they in these roles?

2. Use better ways to find difference makers

At this point in our schema, you have defined your company's critical capabilities and business-critical roles. Now the challenge is to improve your processes for finding and nurturing the top talent that will fill those roles. Most companies rely on two measures, performance and potential, in making hiring, promotion, and succession-planning decisions. They typically incorporate these two factors into the familiar nine-box matrix, with each measure given a high, medium, or low ranking. There's nothing inherently wrong with this construct; it's just that the inputs into the framework and the actions taken as a result lack objectivity, data-driven insight, and meaningful consequences. That renders the whole thing ineffective and a candidate for the scrap heap. Let's look at the problems.

On the performance dimension, a company can make accurate assessments when objective, quantitative data—sales figures, say, or profitability—is readily available. In some cases, performance can't easily be judged by such short-term indicators. However, the larger issue here is that companies may lack the discipline to build a robust, focused set of measurable objectives for employees. These companies instead default to subjective assessments or to objectives that are redefined when it comes time for evaluation. This approach often leads to a perverse kind of grade inflation. A few years ago, for example, we worked with a large state university, which had more than thirteen thousand administrative employees. Each of these employees was evaluated annually on a one-to-five scale, with one meaning "does not meet expectations," three meaning "meets expectations," and five meaning "consistently exceeds expectations." Only seven employees in the previous year had been rated a one or two; more than ten thousand were rated a four or five. Yet leaders repeatedly (and rightly) complained about the university's ability to attract high-quality people to administrative roles.

To avoid grade inflation, some companies implement a forced or stacked ranking system, often known as rank-and-yank.

While these systems dampen grade inflation, they are often too restrictive. More troubling, they can also create an internally competitive work environment, undermining effective teamwork. Many of the more vocal adherents of stacked ranking systems, such as GE and Microsoft, have recently abandoned them.

Another common mistake is to incorporate 360-degree feedback into performance evaluations. This introduces subjectivity and potential gaming into the process—I'll scratch your back if you scratch mine. It's especially toxic when the 360-degree feedback is a factor in determining compensation. And it defeats the purpose of the feedback, which should be aimed at coaching people on future actions rather than evaluating past performance. So it not only corrupts performance measurements; it also weakens your coaching culture. We will have more to say on coaching later in the chapter.

Then there's the "potential" dimension. Measuring potential is more important than measuring performance in hiring decisions. The two are equally important in promotion and career path management. But the task is so fraught with challenges that many organizations have abandoned the attempt, throwing out the nine-box grid in the process. According to a survey of more than a hundred companies by consultancy Talent Strategy Group LLC, managers accurately predict employee potential just over half of the time.[5] Other research comes to similar conclusions, finding that nearly 40 percent of internal job moves made by people identified as high-potential employees end in failure.

Why so bad? One reason is that the assessment of a person's potential is usually inferred, often without sufficient analytical backing. That makes it unnecessarily subjective and, thus, affected by personal biases. A second reason is that the assessment is usually based on the individual's recent performance rather than on his or her longer-term trajectory. In companies that tend to promote rapidly, the results achieved by John and Joan may reflect their predecessors' efforts more than their own, yet John's or Joan's potential is now assessed based on those results. A third reason, and perhaps the most important, relates to who is doing the assessing. Most companies rely on the layer above to assess the layer below. This is problematic if you have B-level players trying to assess A-level talent: they may not recognize it, or if they do, they may resent it.

If companies are so bad at measuring potential despite decades of investing in recruiting and performance evaluation systems, what are they to do about it? Our pragmatic solution comprises four related ideas: behavioral signature, learning agility, collaborative intelligence, and trajectory.

Behavioral signature

This concept rests on two premises.[6] The first is that successful individuals in a company exhibit a distinct behavioral signature, a common way of working that enables them to deliver high performance where others turn in mediocre results. These are not the generic behaviors typically captured in most leadership models; rather, they are ways of acting that are likely to be highly specific to a company and to its strategy, culture, business context, and model. Our second premise is that assessing these behavioral signatures should not be subjective. Data is critical, and modern techniques for analyzing Big Data are useful.

Winning behavioral signatures vary significantly with a company's strategy and culture. Consider the differences between a high-tech company such as Google, say, and an operations- and cost-focused company such as AB InBev, a publicly traded brewer originally backed by the Brazilian founders of 3G Capital, among others. Google defines the talent it wants as "smart creatives." These individuals are "business savvy, data-driven, technically knowledgeable power-users, with creative energy and bias for a hands-on approach." They need to be able to operate autonomously in what Laszlo Bock, chief human resources officer of Google, refers to as a "high freedom" environment. AB InBev uses a different paradigm. As described in the book *Dream Big*—a portrait of 3G and the partners who run it—the brewer wants to attract smart, data-driven, personally hungry, and frugal individuals. They should expect to be highly accountable, and they should be willing to work with constrained resources and proven business routines in an informal and highly demanding environment.' Both companies believe in autonomy but achieve it in different ways. At Google, autonomy is a direct byproduct of agile processes and teams; at AB InBev, autonomy comes from the dramatic elimination of corporate bureaucracy and freedom within a clearly defined framework. So the person who excels at Google and the person who excels at AB InBev will most likely have a different behavioral signature, though they may well possess some similar values and leadership traits.

High-performing companies typically invest heavily in screening for their winning behavioral signature during the interviewing process. Brian Chesky, founder and CEO of Airbnb, personally interviewed the company's first two hundred employees, until it became impractical for him to interview all new hires. In Airbnb's process, job applicants are evaluated for functional and technical skills. Then they undergo two separate culture interviews, during which Airbnb representatives test for six core values. One of these values is "be a host"—that is, show a passion for hospitality and helping people. Airbnb has learned to test for the values and corresponding behaviors through behavioral interviewing techniques and close examination of candidates' backgrounds.

A number of startups have created innovations in the field of developing behavioral signatures. London-based Sinequanon, for example, has developed well-tested techniques for helping companies define the required leadership behavioral signature (trademarked as Performance or Leadership Signature). The company, known as sqn, has also created robust assessment and coaching systems based on periodic feedback; the feedback draws on advanced analytics, proprietary machine learning–artificial intelligence modeling, and intelligent surveying techniques.

Building a leadership development program using sqn's methodology is a three-step process. Step one is to translate your company's strategy into a set of requirements defining the behaviors that make for success, given your company's strategic and cultural context. Part art and part science, this step draws on data-mining techniques and sqn's proprietary database. Step two is to launch a robust 360-degree feedback effort to create a gap assessment for each leader. Leaders are not expected to excel on every facet of the behavioral signature; rather, they are expected to spike in some areas and reach a given threshold in others. As a group, the leadership team should have different spikes but excel on the overall behavioral signature. Step three, finally, is to develop a coaching program, individual interventions, and organizationwide interventions to close the gaps. Only with the right set of interventions, delivered at the right frequency with appropriate reinforcements, will the behavioral change stick.

The experience of a European financial firm illustrates the process. This company, a subsidiary of a larger regional group, is the number-two player in its market, with two retail brands and more than three hundred branches. Though it had been a solid performer in the past, it was facing a rapidly changing market, and new leaders decided that they needed to upgrade their talent. With sqn's help, the firm targeted four hundred leaders and twenty-five hundred total staff for behavioral evaluation and gap assessment.

Figure 4-3 shows the behavioral signature developed for this company. It includes four "energies" labeled "tough love," "inspires," "winner," and "delivers." These attributes were composed of fifteen discrete behaviors and mindsets. The process to develop the signature was critical: it combined senior leaders' judgment, a deep understanding of the industry context, and sqn's database, and it involved employees from the beginning to aid in buy-in. Labels and language were carefully chosen to resonate with the cultural context of the country where the company operated. With the behavioral signature in place, the company could complete the gap identification through an assessment process using sqn's online behavior measurement platform. That data, filtered through an analytical engine, created predictive and actionable feedback. The company also developed tailored online dashboards, to be updated quarterly for each leader.

Rigorous implementation of this process can lead to impressive results. In the European firm's case, productivity growth increased from approximately 5 percent to more than 20 percent. The company moved from bottom quartile to top quartile in terms of overall competitive performance. According to internal surveys, leadership effectiveness increased from 33 percent to 70 percent, while engagement grew from 50 percent to 75 percent.

FIGURE 4-3

Case study of European financial services company

Big Data capability was applied to leadership and culture

Compelling leadership signature
internal graphic

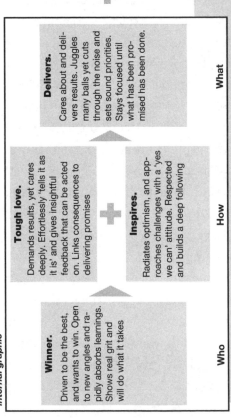

Winner.

Driven to be the best, and wants to win. Open to new angles and rapidly absorbs learnings. Shows real grit and will do what it takes

Tough love.

Demands results, yet cares deeply. Effortlessly 'tells it as it is' and gives insightful feedback that can be acted on. Links consequences to delivering promises

Inspires.

Radiates optimism, and approaches challenges with a 'yes we can' attitude. Respected and builds a deep following

Delivers.

Cares about and delivers results. Juggles many balls yet cuts through the noise and sets sound priorities. Stays focused until what has been promised has been done.

Who   How   What

Analytical engine

- Behavior explains 40%–60% of variability in performance
- Leadership behavior biggest driver of culture (nonlinear relationship)
- Single longitudinal database for all outcome, behavioral, and contextual data

Rigorous data and redesigned 360 feedback
HR workflow

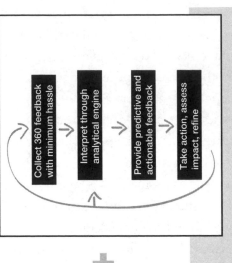

Collect 360 feedback with minimum hassle

Interpret through analytical engine

Provide predictive and actionable feedback

Take action, assess impact, refine

Source: sqn

Although we advocate identifying and screening for your company's winning behavioral signature, we are strong adherents of diversity in all its meanings. Diversity creates the potential for differences in opinion, perspective, insight, and approach. Looking for people who exhibit a certain behavioral DNA should not impede seeking out these differences. Think about a marriage. It's been said that a strong marriage requires enough "sameness" between the partners to allow for compatibility and enough "differentness" to spark passion. In business, sameness creates focus, speed, and alignment, while differentness generates the energy necessary for innovation and evolution. Also, it's important not to confuse the concept of behavioral signatures with personality type. A company or team full of extroverts or alpha males and females is unlikely to be a consistently strong performer. We will touch again on this topic of building diverse, high-potential teams in the following chapter on teaming.

In discussions of human capabilities and behaviors, the debate about how much is shaped by nurture and how much by nature nearly always lurks in the background. We believe that companies can do many things to encourage the kinds of high-performance behaviors that deliver superior business outcomes. But we also believe that many of the actions people take and the behaviors they exhibit reflect deeply ingrained, highly personal beliefs stemming from their backgrounds and genetic makeup. It's hard to make people think or act in a way that is fundamentally different from how they are naturally wired. This is why it's so essential to have a clear view of the behavioral DNA you are in search of, and why it's so important to ensure that difference makers in your organization—the people who will profoundly shape the culture and the outcomes of your business—have some strands of this DNA.

Learning agility

A significant body of empirical research suggests that many high performers are not high potentials, though most high potentials do turn out to be high performers.[8] Whether they do or not depends greatly on their *learning agility*.

Learning agility in our lexicon refers to how quickly individuals adapt to new roles, assimilate new information, and change course or approach based on that new information. At the heart of learning agility are behaviors that allow one to remain open-minded and responsive to data. Another key ingredient is the ability to receive and react constructively to feedback and coaching. The late Chris Argyris, who was a professor at the Harvard Business School, wrote extensively on the challenges related to "teaching smart people how to learn." His research describes the doom loop that intelligent individuals find themselves in if they cannot hear and react to constructive feedback. Argyris's research was conducted decades ago. But the same doom loop is likely to apply to the millennial generation, which grew up in an era when all participants received a trophy and, as in the fictional Lake Wobegon, every child was seen as being above average.

Collaborative intelligence

The term "collaborative intelligence" traces its roots to concepts pioneered in artificial intelligence by thinkers such as Oliver Selfridge.[9] In a business setting, it refers to individuals and groups working autonomously as part of a problem-solving network to create intelligent business outcomes. Success in business obviously requires some degree of collaboration; any organization that expects people to work across functional, geographic, and business-unit boundaries both within their company and as part of a broader business ecosystem depends on their ability to collaborate effectively. But not everyone is equally capable of collaboration, and few companies have explicit systems for helping people learn the skill. Nor do they typically recognize and reward the people who are the strongest collaborators.

Trajectory and hunger

Measuring people's longer-term trajectory based on the distance they have traveled is a stronger indicator of future accomplishments than merely looking at their recent accomplishments. The usual rule is to evaluate someone's performance today and then extrapolate that out into the future. But we think you will get more powerful insights about future performance by examining how much distance people have covered since they started. For instance, future hires who get expensive primary and secondary education and then attend the same Ivy League university as their mothers or fathers will have traveled much less distance than applicants who attended a mediocre public school and university and whose parents never went to college. Which group is likely to be hungrier? Which individuals are likely to achieve more over their lifetimes?

All of these factors—behavioral signature, learning agility, collaborative intelligence, and trajectory and hunger—can be incorporated in quantitative and qualitative measurements of potential. Doing so can help companies dramatically improve their hiring, promotion, and development processes. There remain the questions of where you find candidates—and who should own the talent pipeline.

CEOs with whom we work rarely feel that their talent pipeline is sufficiently robust to consistently meet their companies' future needs. Some believe that only their own company can create the next generation of top talent for business-critical roles. But as markets change and strategies shift, the people who hold key roles today may not be the right people for the future. Loyalty to star performers and contributors is an important part of a healthy culture, but leaving talented people in roles that they can't successfully fill or grow into is a disservice both to them and to the company. Moreover, too great a reliance on internal talent or on past star performers can cause companies to become too insular. They will end up without the expertise, capabilities, and perspectives that can take the company to the next level of performance or challenge the internal conventional wisdom in the interest of business-model innovation. Of course, in other companies, we observe a different extreme. There, it's often assumed that the talent they require will never be grown internally. These companies appear forever enamored of the outside star for hire. A balanced approach to internal talent development and external talent sourcing is key.

Who should take responsibility for the talent pipeline? For external talent, companies often look to HR or executive recruiters for the solution. Leading companies have found that this is almost always a bad idea, especially for the difference makers that they need for business-critical positions. While executive recruiters can sometimes be helpful, they will often find the best available candidate as opposed to the best person for the position, regardless of apparent availability. For example, a rapidly growing software company in Silicon Valley may need talented software engineers and engineering leaders to drive its strategy. These individuals are hard to find. While some of the talent in a headhunter's Rolodex may be quite good, the vast majority are likely to be individuals who have been passed over by the likes of Google, Facebook, Apple, and Salesforce. So, senior executives at many top companies typically take greater ownership for nurturing talent pipelines. Several leading companies, including Bank of America, Pepsi, Dell, and Procter & Gamble, as well as those just mentioned, have built strong in-house recruiting teams. So has our own firm, Bain & Company.

Another useful idea is holding leaders accountable for developing internal difference makers and nurturing networks of external talent. Why not have leaders create personal "talent balance sheets," with assets based on the number and caliber of leaders developed under their watch and liabilities measured by talent they lost or failed to fully develop? It's a recurring theme of this book: human capital needs to be managed as carefully as financial capital. Leaders are responsible for growing human capital over time and so should be held accountable for creating or destroying it.

3. Help make the difference makers even more effective

If you have invested heavily to recruit potential difference makers into your company, you will naturally want to build processes that accelerate their development. This will mean revisiting most of your HR practices and procedures—training, job assignments, compensation, and so on—with that goal in mind. The details are beyond the scope of this book, but by way of illustration, we will give two examples of common practices that likely need to change.

Separate coaching from evaluation

The typical company relies heavily on the traditional annual or semiannual review as its primary coaching and feedback tool for employees. That's a mistake, and many enlightened companies are abandoning these reviews as a primary method for providing employees feedback. Reviews are backward looking and usually fraught with emotion, especially when they are directly linked to compensation. Bosses may be reluctant to provide candid evaluations, given the potential impact on an employee's earnings, and employees may find it difficult to hear the feedback when money is involved. Even more importantly, annual or semiannual reviews can never provide the real-time, in-the-moment coaching that helps individuals understand the context for the feedback. Yet coaching is critical to developing great talent: you want to create an environment in which individuals are challenged to learn and grow, and where they are helped to do so by more experienced people. That's why many high-performing companies have completely separated their performance appraisal and coaching processes, often guided by a simple framework like that shown in figure 4-4. Most of these companies have also built coaching systems and trained managers to be effective coaches through more frequent feedback and real-time guidance.

*Accelerate talent development through
smarter rotations*

Nearly every large company tries to manage assignments and rotations as part of its career development process. But rotation can be tough to get right. For example, the conventional assignment is usually no more than two years long, and results may

FIGURE 4-4

Separating coaching from evaluation is critical

	Focus	Measure	Linkage to rewards	Frequency	Leadership's role
Evaluate	• The "what"	• Outcomes	• Meritocratic • Meaningful consequences	• Semiannual performance reviews	• Establish objectives • Determine performance
Coach	• The "how"	• Behaviors, methods, and style	• Never	• Daily and real-time coaching sessions	• Role model behaviors • Coach each individual to personal full potential

Source: Bain & Company

take more time than that to materialize. So individuals can be unfairly penalized or rewarded for results that stem largely from their predecessor's actions. Not only does this make performance assessment challenging; it also has deleterious effects on an individual's professional development. He or she doesn't get the benefit of feedback to see what works, what doesn't, and what corrective action might be necessary to return the company to the right course. We asked executives in our survey how often they thought their companies got talent rotations right. These managers believed that they got the assignment duration appropriate just a little over 50 percent of the time.

In our experience, the optimal assignment length runs closer to three years than two years. But you may want to tell people that they have a multiyear mission with well-defined milestones and measurable accomplishments, rather than set a fixed period. The job description can explicitly describe this multiyear objective, one of which must always be to identify a pool of successors. In ordinary circumstances, employees placed in business-critical roles under these conditions shouldn't be considered for new assignments until they have successfully completed their multiyear missions.

LinkedIn

LinkedIn illustrates many of these themes. The company—acquired by Microsoft in June 2016 for $26 billion—is a fast-growing organization with big talent requirements that just happens to be in the business of talent. In the words of founder Reid Hoffman, its mission is to help its millions of members "change their own economic curve by the strength of their alliances and connections with other people." It's also about helping people use their time more effectively and efficiently. "We used to say," Hoffman commented, "that the difference in types of social [media] is this: is your point to waste time or to gain time? [Entertainment-focused] social networks are about spending time, and what makes you spend time? Well, it has to be entertaining. But we wanted to help people accomplish critical tasks in a shorter amount of time."

How LinkedIn finds difference makers. Talent is LinkedIn's top operating priority. The traits of people CEO Jeff Weiner says he most enjoys working with are similar to what LinkedIn looks for in new hires:

- **The ability to dream big.** Weiner wants people to have a vision that inspires others and that can push the company forward.

- **The ability to execute ("get shit done," in LinkedIn's vernacular).** People should be able to break down that vision into the parts required to get it done, overcoming objections through resourcefulness and, as Weiner puts it, "sheer force of will."

- **The ability to have fun.** LinkedIn's difference makers should help make the workplace fun. "Jerks" wouldn't fit in even if they are visionary and can execute.

Weiner captures these elements in the Venn diagram shown in figure 4-5.

How LinkedIn keeps difference makers engaged and motivated. LinkedIn's concept of a mutually beneficial employment agreement based on a "tour of duty" is one of the most powerful tools we have seen for talent development, retention, and

FIGURE 4-5

Weiner's Venn diagram of people he most enjoys working with

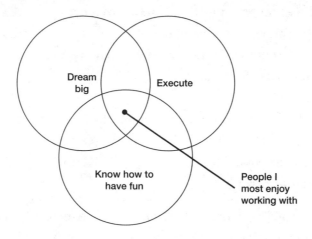

Source: Jeff Weiner, CEO, LinkedIn, linkedin.com.

engagement. Here's how Hoffman and his coauthors define the concept in their book *The Alliance*:

> When Reid first founded LinkedIn, for example, he offered an explicit deal to talented employees. If they signed up for a tour of duty of between two to four years and made an important contribution to some part of the business, Reid and the company would help advance their careers, preferably in the form of another tour of duty at LinkedIn. This approach worked: the company got an engaged employee who worked to achieve tangible results for LinkedIn and who could be an advocate and resource for the company if he chose to leave after one or more tours of duty.
>
> The employee transformed his career by enhancing his portfolio of skills and experiences. By recasting careers at your company as a series of successive tours of duty, you

can better attract and retain entrepreneurial employees. When recruiting top talent, offering a clear tour of duty with specific benefits and success outcomes beats vague promises like "you'll get valuable experience." Defining an attractive tour of duty lets you point to concrete ways that it will enhance the employee's personal brand—while he's at the company and if and when he works elsewhere—by integrating a specific mission, picking up real skills, building new relationships, and so on.[10]

Chances are your most talented employees already spend considerable time thinking about next steps to pursue their passions and develop their careers. Creating time-bounded missions focused on a defined set of outcomes is a powerful way not only to align interests but also to create a natural structure for re-recruiting talented people for their next mission—as opposed to simply reacting when another opportunity drops in their lap.

How LinkedIn helps difference makers become better. The company also invests in a broad range of initiatives to help its talented people grow and develop. The measures include the following.

- LinkedIn encourages employees to build their personal networks *outside* the company by allocating time and resources for this purpose. Perhaps it's not surprising that an organization whose business is helping professionals build their networks would do the same for its employees, but the benefits accrue both to individuals and to the company. Employees increase their career value by enhancing their networks and exposing themselves to new ideas. In return, the company gets employees who feel trusted and inspired, and who can leverage their networks for the company's benefit.

- Once a month, LinkedIn holds what it calls an Investment Day, or "InDay" for short. Employees worldwide set aside their regular work to explore new ideas for personal and professional development.

- LinkedIn also creates a culture that values "transformation." Company executives talk regularly about transformation from three perspectives: transformation of self, transformation of company, and transformation of the world. The goal of transformation of self is to leave LinkedIn a better professional than when you started. The company facilitates this through programs such as a speaker series, wellness programs, and a sizable training budget. The goal of transformation of the company is to help LinkedIn realize its full potential; relevant actions include an initiative called Women in Tech, diversity programs, and biweekly all-hands meetings. The goal of transformation of world is to create economic opportunity for every member of the global workforce. That means digitally mapping the world economy and connecting talent with opportunity on a global scale; supporting LinkedIn for Good, which connects professionals with opportunities to work for change; and using InDays to volunteer for special causes. Transformation as a concept is critical for a company whose business is highly talent dependent and whose business model is centered on a dynamic, digitally enabled professional network. Building a culture of continuous transformation ensures that the organization's internal environment is as dynamic as the external one.

LinkedIn's value as a professional network is amplified in a world where lifetime employment is mostly a thing of the past, where talent is mobile, and where a company's scarcest resources are time, talent, and energy. The founders put it this way:

> Members come first. That's our top value. Normally in a business, your customers are your top priority because they are the ones that are paying you money. Here, our members are the most important thing, even though only a small number are paying us money. That's because we are building a lifelong relationship through which we are trying to help them change their career trajectories.

While LinkedIn aspires to retain top talent and engage these individuals in transformational missions, the company's leaders realize that lifetime employment is no longer a realistic ambition. In this sense, the organization follows the same advice it gives to corporate clients, treating its alumni network as a key asset. That reinforces LinkedIn's business model, employee value proposition, purpose, and culture. What's more, it all seems to work. In a study of talent flows in the tech industry, the recruitment website Top Prospect found that LinkedIn is able to hire 7.5 people for every employee it loses to competitors—a number that compares favorably with Google (1.2) and is in the same ballpark as talent magnet Facebook (8.1).

Finding and developing your A-level talent is an essential element in overcoming organizational drag. Interestingly, though, the top-quartile companies in our survey had only a little more top talent than the other companies. In short, there was little difference on this score between the best and the rest. What made the biggest difference on the talent front—and it was sizable—was where the top companies focused their difference makers and, as we'll see, how they *teamed* and *deployed* their best talent. Let's turn to that topic now.

THREE KEYS TO FINDING AND DEVELOPING MORE DIFFERENCE MAKERS

1. *Determine where difference makers can truly make a difference.* Link your talent plan to your value-creation strategy; skew resources to the areas where you are trying to build competitive advantage. Define the 100 to 150 key positions, and fill them with difference makers. Never accept the premise that talent must dilute as you grow, especially for these roles.

2. *Upgrade your techniques for finding difference makers, and hold your leaders accountable for developing them.* Translate your strategy and culture into a behavioral signature. Incorporate learning agility, collaborative intelligence, and trajectory and hunger into your measurements for leadership potential. Ultimately, senior leaders must own the talent plan, not HR and not executive recruiters.

3. *Help your difference makers become even better.* Revisit your HR practices. Invest in data-driven coaching that helps talented individuals further develop these behavioral traits. Take a fresh look at your talent-rotation strategy and make sure to avoid the twin pitfalls of under- and over-rotation.

5

Create and Deploy
All-Star Teams

Few people in business work alone. Even a company's A-level players, its difference makers, must collaborate with others to accomplish anything. Given that obvious truth, it's remarkable how little attention most companies pay to collaboration, teaming, and deployment. When they need to get something important done, they throw bodies at the problem. Some assemble teams based on no criterion other than who happens to be available. Others make a point of assembling "balanced" teams, with a mixture of star, middling, and poor performers, probably in hopes that the top players will bring the others up to their level. But somehow it never seems to work out that way.[1]

The stakes here are sizable, because the performance gaps that separate a company's difference makers from the rest of its workforce are magnified through teaming. Great teams act as a kind of force multiplier. They allow people—particularly top performers—to achieve more than they ever thought they could. Take, for example, the US Navy's special operations teams, known as Seals. Navy Seals are extraordinary soldiers—each is more than ten times as destructive as the average soldier on the battlefield. But create a team of ten Navy Seals and you get far more than 100 times the destructive power of an average soldier—more like 150 or even 200 times. That's why the United States relies on Seal teams to carry out critical security missions, from the termination of Osama bin Laden in 2011 to the rescue of Jessica Buchanan and Poul Hagen Thisted from Somali pirates in 2012.

Companies that create great teams and ensure effective collaboration within and between teams dramatically outperform their peers. Consider just two examples:

- SpaceX, Elon Musk's rocket design and manufacturing company, developed its Falcon 9 Launch Vehicle for just under $1.7 billion. NASA's own associate deputy administrator for policy estimates that it would have cost the agency (and the American taxpayer) nearly $4 billion to match this achievement—close to 135 percent more. One big difference according to NASA: SpaceX relied on many fewer people. Its engineers worked long hours, probably longer than their NASA counterparts would have. But even more important was the efficiency and productivity of SpaceX's top-performing design teams, which developed and launched the rocket for a fraction of what it would have cost NASA.[2]

- The blockbuster movie *Toy Story*—the top-grossing film of 1995, and a movie widely considered to have transformed animated storytelling—wasn't the product of a single visionary filmmaker. Rather, it was the result of an often prickly but ultimately productive collaboration among Pixar's top artists and animators, Disney's veteran executives (including Jeffrey Katzenberg, then head of the film division), and Steve Jobs. The Pixar team originally presented Disney with what Katzenberg deemed an uninspiring tale.[3] A major revision—far more edgy, at Katzenberg's insistence—lacked the cheeriness essential to a family movie. Finally, the group came up with something that satisfied everyone on the team, and that would later be dubbed by *Time* magazine "the year's most inventive comedy."[4] Pixar—which is managed as a separate unit within Disney—has continued to set records with its team-based approach. Virtually all of its movies have been hits, and all but two have outgrossed the original *Toy Story*'s $374 million. This list includes *Finding Nemo* and its sequel, *Finding Dory*, both with about $900 million gross revenue; *Inside Out*, with $857 million; and of course the two sequels to *Toy Story*, the most recent of which topped $1 billion.

Not every company, of course, is in an entrepreneurial or creative business like these, and not every company can organize itself in the manner of SpaceX or Pixar. But any organization can take advantage of the power of great teams and collaboration to produce extraordinary results. Indeed, companies need to do so if they are not to waste the effort they put into eliminating organizational drag and finding and cultivating great talent. This chapter shows how.

All-star teams

A key step any company can take to supercharge performance is to create teams of its top players—we call them all-star teams—and deploy them against its mission-critical initiatives.

These teams will produce more results and produce them faster than average teams.

This recommendation is surprisingly unconventional. The usual wisdom, after all, is that all-star teams just don't work. Egos will take over. The stars won't play well with one another and will drive the team leader crazy. But it's time to reconsider those assumptions. When the stakes are high—when a business model needs to be reinvented, say, or a key new product designed, or a strategic problem solved—doesn't it seem foolish not to put your best people on the job, provided you can find a way to manage them effectively?

We have seen all-star teams do extraordinary work. For example, it took just six hundred Apple engineers less than two years to develop, debug, and deploy OS X, a revolutionary change in the company's operating system. By contrast, it took as many as ten thousand engineers more than five years to develop, debug, deploy, and eventually retract Windows Vista. There were important strategic differences between Apple and Microsoft, of course. But based on our research and on interviews with executives at both companies, we're convinced that the approach the two companies took to teaming and deployment explains a significant portion of the almost fiftyfold difference in productivity.

Common sense suggests that all-star teams have at least two big advantages: sheer firepower and synergy.

Sheer firepower. If you have world-class talent of all kinds on a team, you multiply the productivity and performance advantages that stand-alone stars can deliver. Consider autoracing pit crews. Kyle Busch's six-man crew is widely considered the finest on the NASCAR circuit. Each member is the best for his position—gas man, jackman, tire carriers, and tire changers. Crew members train together year-round with one clear goal in mind: to get Busch's #18 racer in and out of the pit in the shortest possible time. The crew can execute a standard pit stop—seventy-three maneuvers including refueling and a change of all four tires—in 12.12 seconds. Add just one average player to Busch's crew—say, an ordinary tire changer—and that time nearly doubles, to 23.09 seconds. Add two average team members to the mix, and it climbs to well over half a minute. By implication, then, the impact that all-star teams have on productivity is geometric, not linear.[5] As the percentage of A-level players on a team increases, the output of the team increases geometrically.

Synergy. But it's not just the quantity of team output that is affected by all-star teams. The quality of output improves as well. Putting the best thinkers together can spur creativity and ideas that no one member of the team would have developed alone. When Mickey Drexler was turning around Gap Inc. in the 1990s, he built powerful product-merchandising capabilities by assembling a merchant and design core team comprising the best of the best. Recognizing that great product is the lifeblood of great performance in retail, he and his team identified the company's most talented product merchants and designers based on each employee's track record, both inside and outside the company. Then they created a team of exclusively A-level players. (Many members of this core team have gone on to run highly successful retail operations, including Maureen Chiquet, former CEO at Chanel, and Andy Janowski, formerly of Burberry and Smythson.) Drexler tasked this team with translating his vision into specific products for every season, for each of the company's stores.

The results were impressive. The team executed one of the most successful turnarounds in retail history, transforming Gap into the leading retailer of own-brand merchandise. It also produced great results for the company's shareholders. Between 1998 and 2001, Gap was the most successful retailer in the United States, growing far faster and creating more value than any other retail brand.

The ability of all-star teams to produce more and higher-quality output is what we call the force multiplier. The impact on performance can be dramatic. Think about the difference between a professional basketball team and an amateur team. Both groups can play the game, but pit them against one another on the court and you are likely to see a ten- to twentyfold difference in the number of points scored by the pros versus the amateurs.

Mission-critical initiatives

At any given point in time, every company has—or should have—a list of its most important priorities. These initiatives will determine the company's future prospects; they are the tasks that must be completed successfully if the company is to survive and prosper. The list may include integrating a major merger, developing a new product line, or even redefining the company's basic strategy and direction (as IBM, say, has done over the past several years). Whatever the specifics, these are the priorities for all-star teams to tackle. They are the arenas where teams of difference makers can have the biggest effect.

Our research and experience highlight an important contrast in the approach companies take to assembling and deploying teams against their mission-critical initiatives. In our survey, for example, about 75 percent of the leaders of the best-performing companies said that they used all-star teams whenever their organization launched an initiative considered critical to business success. The comparable figure for the remaining companies was less than 10 percent—a more than sevenfold difference. Just as significant, bottom performers in our survey were four times as likely as the best to assemble and deploy teams based on who was available.

You can see the impact of all-star teams at key moments in recent business history. In 1990, for example, Boeing recognized that it had a gap in its product lineup: it had no airplane positioned between the jumbo 747 jetliner and its midsized 767 model. To address this gap, the company assembled a team of its best engineers. The team was led first by Phil Condit, who went on to became CEO of Boeing, and then by Alan Mulally, later CEO of Ford.

The all-star team came up with a design effort that was different from anything the company had previously employed. Team members worked with eight major airlines—All Nippon, American, British Airways, Cathay Pacific, Delta, JAL, Qantas, and United—to design the aircraft, the first time customers were so deeply involved in the process. They also designed the 777 wholly on the computer, the first airplane to be designed electronically. Using in-depth customer input and employing the latest technology, the team completed the basic design for the 777 in less than four months, and the company had the plane ready for service in less than five years, nearly two years faster than any other previous program. By bringing together its engineering stars and having them work side-by-side with customers, Boeing was able to launch what many industry analysts view as the most successful airplane program in commercial aviation history (with nearly 950 in service today), and to do it faster than ever before.

More recently, the turnaround at Ford between 2006 and 2010 serves as a powerful example of the impact of teaming. In 2006, though the economy was booming, Ford was struggling. The company's North American operations were generating sizable losses as consumer preferences moved away from Ford's profitable trucks and SUVs toward smaller vehicles, a segment where the majority of the company's products were unprofitable. Bill Ford, then the company's chairman and CEO, assembled an all-star team comprising Mark Fields (later Ford CEO), Bob Shanks (later CFO), Joe Hinrichs (later president of Ford Americas), and others, to devise a "Way Forward Plan" for the North America division. The plan the team came up with was ambitious: it included shutting down underutilized manufacturing plants and renegotiating labor agreements with the UAW. When Mulally joined Ford as CEO in 2006, he reinforced and broadened the Way Forward Plan, taking on billions of dollars in additional debt, shedding noncore brands (Aston Martin, Jaguar, Land Rover, Volvo, Mazda), and investing in new and revamped cars such as the Focus, Fusion, and Fiesta. In just three years, Ford North America went from losing more than $4 billion a year to making more than $5 billion.

Today, a handful of leading companies are building this model of all-star teams versus mission-critical initiatives into their day-to-day management. The Dell management model, for example, identifies the company's highest-priority strategic initiatives and ensures that leaders' time and the company's best talent are focused on making these initiatives a success. Each year, Dell creates an agenda made up of the company's highest value at stake and most urgent issues and opportunities. It usually includes fewer than fifteen items. Leadership team meetings then review the relevant facts and data associated with each issue, formulate concrete alternatives, evaluate options, and make choices. A senior executive and a team of A-level players are then assigned to help Dell's top management address each issue on the agenda. This management approach focuses leaders on mission-critical issues and ensures that all-star teams are deployed to capitalize on the company's most promising opportunities.

Making all-star teams work

Creating effective all-star teams can be a dicey proposition. Many executives can cite examples of star performers who fought with one another and didn't get much done. But under the right conditions, all-star teams can turn in extraordinary results. Let's look at how to help them live up to their potential.

Great leadership. The most important variable, and one that many companies overlook, is who leads the team. Leaders themselves have to be A-level talent, capable of coaxing top performance out of their team members. If you were assembling a chamber orchestra made up of the world's best players—think Itzhak Perlman, Gil Shaham, Yuri Bashmet, Yo-Yo Ma, and their peers—you wouldn't put an amateur conductor in front of them. Business is no different. It was no accident that both Gap's and Boeing's all-star teams were led by individuals who themselves were difference makers.

Organizations thus need to invest as much time in picking team leaders as in picking members. They need to ask members for feedback on the leader early (and often), and they can't be afraid to switch generals or even to promote a team member to leader when necessary. In a 2012 study of a large company's front-line supervisors, the National Bureau of Economic Research concluded that, as one summary put it, "The most efficient structure is to assign the best workers to the best bosses."[6] The research found that a great boss can improve the productivity of any team. Put an A-level boss (one in the top 10 percent in leader quality) instead of a poor boss in charge of an average team and she will increase the productivity of the team by 10 percent—about the same as adding another member to a nine-member team. But put that same A-level boss in charge of an all-star team and the team's productivity will increase by still more: "good bosses . . . increase the output of stars by more than they do of laggards," say the researchers. Because of the force multiplier, the performance of the all-star team will be much higher than that of an average team. So great bosses, in effect, act as a force multiplier on the force multiplier of all-star teams.[7]

This kind of leadership ability is a rare commodity, and it may be hard to find enough A-level leaders to head up your all-star teams. One CEO with whom we recently worked told us, "We are fortunate enough to have plenty of 'A' talent to deploy against our critical efforts. But our rate-limiting factor is leadership. We have only nine 'A' leaders who can drive these teams." The CEO's solution: create nine all-star teams and put them on the top-priority initiatives; then have the teams move down the list as they completed each one. These teams were so much more productive than the company's other teams that they still got through the list faster than a group of balanced teams could have.

Leverage "extra-milers." Every organization has employees who will go the extra mile. Committed and engaged, they invest extra time and energy in making critical initiatives successful, often contributing well beyond the scope of their role. These extra-milers can play an essential role in team collaboration. They serve as the productive glue between individual team members, helping to keep everyone informed and working together effectively. Research by the University of Iowa's Ning Li and coauthors found that a single extra-miler can increase team productivity by more than the other members of the team combined.[8]

Identifying these extra-milers and assigning them to all-star teams serves to knit team members together. They provide the assists that enable the all-stars on the team to score more points. Every great team needs an extra-miler to help it function and perform in top form.

The right incentives—and no disincentives. Companies relying on all-star teams need to track and reward team performance, not just individual accomplishment. But some companies' performance assessment methods get in the way of team success. Microsoft is an example: for many years, the software giant used a "stacked ranking" system as part of its performance evaluation model. At regular intervals, a certain percentage of any team's members would be rated "top performers," "good," "average," "below average," and "poor," regardless of the team's overall performance. In some situations, this kind of forced ranking is effective, but in Microsoft's case, it had unintended consequences. Over time, according to insiders' reports, the stacked ranking created a culture in which employees competed with one another, rather than against other companies. Top performers rarely liked to join groups with other A-level players, because they feared they might be seen as the weakest members of the team. A-level players at Microsoft, so the story goes, were those who could identify B-level and C-level players and get themselves teamed with them, thus maximizing the odds of rating near the top of the stacked rank.[9]

Great support. To do their best, all-star teams need support staff who are all-stars, too. Extremely talented people have often never worked for someone they can learn a lot from; in our experience, most relish the opportunity and pull out all the stops. And high-caliber subordinates allow team members to accomplish more. A gifted administrative assistant, for example, requires less direction and competently shoulders many routine tasks, so the other team members can focus on what they do best.

Big goals to neutralize big egos. Egos can get in the way of team performance. But they don't have to. In 1992, America's first "Dream Team"—made up of the very best basketball players in the NBA—swept the Olympic Games in Barcelona, defeating its opponents by an average of forty-four points. This team succeeded because the goal of representing the United States with honor at the Olympics was bigger than even the sometimes oversized egos of these talented players. Again, the business lesson is clear. Since you can't put all-star teams on every job—there aren't enough A-level players to go around— you want to save these teams for the mission-critical tasks, and make sure every member understands the tasks' importance. The teams at Gap, Boeing, and SpaceX were doing jobs that would determine the future of those companies. If you want your top performers to work productively together, you have to inspire them to put the mission first. In effect, the "collective ego" needs to become bigger than any one player's individual ego.

Avoiding overshadowing. One danger of relying on all-star teams is that it creates a kind of star system, in which the top players get outsize rewards, while everyone else feels undervalued. Since an organization depends on all its participants, not just the top performers, that result can undermine the beneficial impact of the all-stars. One antidote is to ensure that everyone shares in the A-level team's achievements. George Clooney and the rest of the all-star cast in the movie *Ocean's Eleven* created an environment in which cast and crew reveled in their mutual success. Reportedly, most crew members were so pleased with the experience that they sought to sign on for *Ocean's Twelve* and *Ocean's Thirteen*. Other ways to keep B-level players and others engaged include recognizing performance, whether it's mission critical or not; using a common performance evaluation system for stars and nonstars; and establishing common rewards shared by all. We discuss some of these methods at greater length in chapters 4 and 6.

Promoting productive teamwork

Not every team at your company can be an all-star team. Since exceptional talent is a scarce commodity, there will always be a limit on the number of all-star teams any company can assemble and deploy. So, many of your teams will necessarily include B-level and C-level players. Countless books and articles have been written on how to make these everyday teams as productive as they can be, and we won't try to repeat all their prescriptions here. We believe, however, that the lessons of all-star teams apply to other teams as well. Every team needs a respected, competent leader. Every team needs appropriate support and the right incentives.

We want to add a final note of caution. "Collaboration" has become a buzzword in business these days. Employees are encouraged to communicate with their coworkers frequently, work across organizational silos, access the "wisdom of the crowd," and so on. Much of this is good advice. But when it comes to collaboration and teamwork, more is not always better. Research featured in *Harvard Business Review* in 2016 noted that the amount of time devoted to collaborative activities has ballooned by 50 percent or more over the last several years. Not all of this additional time has produced bottom-line results; much of it has been wasted on needless meetings, unnecessary emails, and so forth, as we have highlighted earlier in this book. Moreover, value-added collaboration—collaboration that actually advances the cause of an individual or team—is highly concentrated in very few employees. Research on three hundred organizations found that, in most cases, 20 percent to 35 percent of value-added collaboration comes from only 3 percent to 5 percent of employees. As demands on these individuals mount, collaboration overload sets in, leading to higher turnover and, ironically, less value-added collaboration over time. At the same time, what Cal Newport of Georgetown University calls "deep work" suffers. People spend so much time working in teams that they have no time left for uninterrupted concentration on critical tasks.[10]

So think about teaming in the spirit of this book. Make sure that every team you set up is really necessary—and that the costs aren't higher than the anticipated benefits. With all-star teams, the odds are high that you will get what you pay for. And more.

Hiring great talent—difference makers—puts a company on the road toward overcoming the effects of organizational drag. Assembling that great talent into all-star teams moves it a lot farther down that road, because all-star teams outperform other teams so dramatically. If you can make these teams work well, they will address your company's mission-critical initiatives and so help it survive and prosper.

Now it's time to move on to part three of this book, which looks at the organizationwide issues of employee engagement, inspiration, and culture.

THREE WAYS TO CREATE AND DEVELOP ALL-STAR TEAMS

1. *Form teams of your best people.* Teams of A-level players do things better and faster than mixed teams. They act as a force multiplier.

2. *Put these teams on your organization's most impor-tant issues.* Since there aren't enough A-level players for everything, you need to focus the all-star teams on mission-critical initiatives, those that will determine the future value of the company.

3. *Manage these teams carefully.* All-star teams need great leaders and great support. You need to offer them the right incentives, and to ensure that egos don't interfere with collaboration.

PART THREE

ENERGY

The company is us. I mean myself and 100,000
other colleagues of mine. If we're excited, knowing
what we want to do, aligned, inspired, moving
forward, learning, attracting better people than
we are, all the time, [then] the company is moving
in that direction. It's progressing. It's growing.

—Carlos Brito, CEO, AB InBev

N o one ever washes a rental car.

Unless you feel real ownership—real connection—you will never devote the extra energy needed to make something better. The same is true in business. Unless your employees feel engaged, even inspired, by the work they are doing, they will not invest their discretionary energy in the company, its customers, or its success.

In this part of the book, we introduce the third factor affecting performance. As it turns out, organizational energy is the single most powerful factor we measured, raising the average company twenty-four points on the productivity index.

Energy is intangible, but we all know it when we see it. Engaged employees bring commitment and enthusiasm to their work and apply it to their jobs every day. Some companies' cultures seem almost to generate energy. And high-energy organizations can accomplish amazing things. (Ever check out the "Best Places to Work" lists? Most of those companies deliver dramatically better financial results than others.) Engagement and a strong culture multiply the impact of your company's two scarcest resources, time and talent. They allow you to punch above your weight, to accomplish more with less.

Chapter 6 focuses on engagement, which has been an intractable problem for most companies. Our survey found that the average company engages barely a third of its workforce and must put up with nearly a tenth who are actively dissatisfied. While we expected to see engagement correlated with productivity, we were surprised by two things. One was the size of the multiplier: engagement really makes a difference. The other was the gains that come from what our respondents saw as *inspired* employees. The survey indicates that inspired employees are 90 percent more productive than engaged employees, and more than twice as productive as employees who are merely satisfied.

Chapter 7 goes on to examine culture. A great culture creates employee energy; a toxic one destroys it. Think back to how you felt every time you started a new job or a new assignment. You were full of optimism about what you could accomplish. Some companies manage to sustain that kind of spirit through people's entire careers. Every day brings new challenges and opportunities, and your energy builds over time as you work with other talented people to accomplish more than you thought possible. In other companies, alas, the new-employee spirit vanishes within weeks. Chapter 7 will show how the best companies' cultures channel employees' energy to achieve remarkable outcomes—and how you can reawaken that kind of culture in your company.

6

Aim for Inspiration (Not Just Engagement)

"You don't need any fancy surveys to know how engaged your employees are," a client of ours once told us. "Just look at the parking lot."

We must have looked puzzled, because the client felt he had to explain: "Walk around the parking lot in late morning. Count the number of cars that are backed in to their spaces. If employees take the time to back in just so they can make a faster exit at the end of the day, they're probably counting the minutes until the workday ends. It's like they need a getaway car to escape the scene of a crime."

The real crime, of course, is the creation of organizations where people have no passion for the work they do every day. Instead of being advocates for their companies and their careers there, they are hostages to a paycheck. In the Bain–Economist Intelligence Unit study, we examined employee engagement in more than three hundred companies across twelve industry sectors. The data captured in figure 6-1 presents a

FIGURE 6-1

Employee engagement is a problem in every industry

Employee engagement by industry (percent)

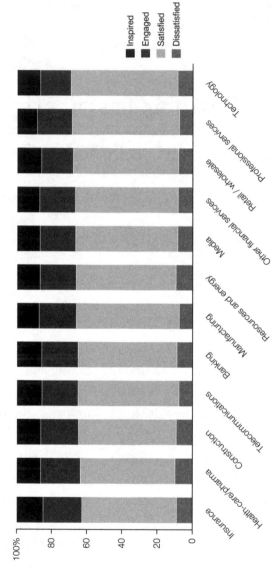

■ Inspired
■ Engaged
▨ Satisfied
▨ Dissatisfied

Source: Bain/EIU research (N=308).

sad picture about the state of engagement in companies worldwide. No wonder people want to get home when the proverbial whistle blows.

It isn't hard to figure out why engagement is so low. Many of today's complex organizations have become soul-crushing institutions. Employees in such places have little autonomy. Their work is rote and routinized, often micromeasured and micromanaged. Companies aspire to link their employees' jobs to the organization's higher purpose, but the daily grind makes these aspirations feel disingenuous or unreachable. Many employees don't believe that they are learning and growing in their jobs. And they feel so disconnected from colleagues and teams that day-to-day interactions seem more like transactions than helpful collaborations.

The price of disengagement is high. Employees in these environments will give a company little of their discretionary energy—why would they give more?—so productivity suffers. All that micromanagement is usually counterproductive from the company's point of view as well. It's expensive and time consuming. And no one has yet figured out how to micromanage employees into coming up with great ideas, willingly going the extra mile for a customer, collaborating selflessly with peers, or adapting quickly to a changing marketplace. Yet these are the skills most companies require in today's world.

In response to such concerns, many organizations have tried hard to boost employee engagement. They tinker with compensation, incentives, benefit packages, surveys and other methods of feedback, training programs, off-site excursions, and all the other techniques in the human resources toolkit. These actions generally have little effect on engagement; if they did, the numbers wouldn't have remained so stubbornly low for so many years. What's missing?

Our experience in both high- and low-energy organizations has repeatedly taught us a simple lesson, which we will develop in this chapter. Companies are aiming too low. The real breakthrough in energy comes not just from engagement but from employees who feel *inspired* by their jobs and the organization they work for. Inspired employees are themselves far more productive than average employees or even engaged employees, as the statistics in our survey suggest. They become difference makers. And inspiration is contagious, so they also inspire those around them to strive for greater heights. In the workplace, as one pundit put it, employees react differently when they encounter a wall. Satisfied employees hold a meeting to discuss what to do about walls. Engaged employees begin looking around for ladders to scale the wall. Inspired employees just break right through it.

To be sure, people are different, and you can't expect everyone on the payroll to feel inspired. But if you aim high—if you aim to build a company that inspires as many people as possible—you will win over many hearts and minds, and you are far more likely to end up with a sizable percentage of employees who are at least engaged.

Research—our own and others'—sharpens the distinction between engagement and inspiration. People typically become engaged with their work through one of three methods. They may be attached to the content of the work itself. They may feel engaged because of connections to people—the bosses they work for and the teams they work with. They may believe in the company's purpose. (We'll have more to say on that kind of attachment in the following chapter.) While it always is better to have employees attached in at least one of these ways—that's what creates engagement—the deeply inspired employee is attached in all three. If you are to be truly inspired in your job, for example, it's not enough to like the content of your work but not your employer or the people you work with. Truly great places to work create all three sorts of engagement: they translate a company's purpose into the content of people's work, and they nurture inspirational bosses and high-performing teams that help individuals reach their own full potential.

The impact on productive power is significant. When we asked senior executives in our survey about the productivity of inspired employees, they estimated that an inspired employee is more than twice as productive as a merely satisfied one. These estimates jibe with the experience of companies that we have advised. Dell Technologies, for example, has been tracking employee satisfaction and engagement for many years. Since 2014, Steve Price, Dell's senior vice president for human resources, and his team have modified the company's "Tell Dell" survey to better measure employee (and team) inspiration. The data is, well, telling. Employees who are inspired by their leadership and work at Dell are 30 percent more likely to recommend Dell's products to a family member or friend compared to employees who are merely satisfied. They are three times as likely to recommend Dell as a place to work, and the referrals they do make are nearly twice as likely to be hired and stay on. They themselves are half as likely to leave Dell for job opportunities elsewhere. The impact of employee inspiration goes beyond advocacy for the company's products, services, and job opportunities. Direct sales teams led by leaders rated as inspiring sell 6 percent more on average than sales teams led by uninspiring leaders. If the company could convert uninspiring leaders into inspiring ones—and if this ratio held up—Dell could generate more than $1 billion in additional revenues each year.

There is a rich body of other research from behavioral psychologists, business school academics, and consultant-practitioners regarding specific techniques for engaging your workforce. In what follows, we won't attempt to cover this broad landscape. Rather, we offer a pragmatist's formula showing how a senior leadership team can take dramatic steps toward increasing inspirational engagement through a few simple ideas. Companies that inspire their employees start with a *humane philosophy of the workplace*, and they develop the ability to put that philosophy into practice through their operating model, talent systems, employee value proposition, and ways of working. They foster *autonomy*, perhaps the most important single element in inspiration. Many companies compromise people's autonomy, usually because they are (rightly) concerned with broader organizational goals such as repeatability and scalability. But it's possible to balance these objectives, as we will see. Finally, they *develop inspiring leaders*, individuals who can build an organization that both performs and inspires others. As we discuss in the following chapter, performance and inspiration create a virtuous circle. Inspiring leadership is the first step to getting this virtuous circle started—and it's within reach of all of your leaders.

These fundamentals go a long way toward creating an environment where people actively *want* to work. Such an environment is your best recruiter, your best retention policy, and your best route to engagement: it re-recruits the entire workforce every day, and it gives them a reason to care deeply about what they do. Let's look at each of the three elements.

1. Develop and implement a humane philosophy

A good starting point is to ask yourself a question. What kind of environment would you like to work in? You would probably want to know your group's mission, and your own. You would want to know how those missions were connected to the company's purpose. You would want to eliminate all of the organizational drag that makes it hard for people to get their jobs done every day.

Most of the leaders we talk to have other ambitions as well for their organization. They want to build teams of high-performing individuals, and they want to give those teams considerable autonomy to complete their missions. They want to create a place where employees can grow to whatever level their ambition and abilities take them. They understand that some of these employees will seek mastery, while others will just want to be good at their job and get better every day. But they want everyone to feel a part of the organization and to identify with its goals.

This kind of environment isn't a myth; you can see it in operation at many of the "millennial" companies that have come into being in the last few decades—companies such as Google, Netflix, Spotify, Airbnb, Tesla, SpaceX, and many others. Most of these companies have business models that are supercharged by digital technologies. Many are led by their founders and exhibit the traits of what our colleagues Chris Zook and James Allen have termed the "founder's mentality." They often seem successful in engaging their people in pursuit of a bold mission. How do they do it?

- **They set out to make a difference.** They are results oriented, and they often have a David-versus-Goliath attitude that makes them fiercely competitive. They express their goals not just in terms of business success, but also in terms of the impact they have on the lives of their customers and on the larger society. At Dell, for example, leaders emphasize "the next billion people that will have access to education; the next billion who will receive better medical care based on the information Dell makes available to doctors." It's big goals like these that motivate employees to go the extra mile.

- **They presume trust.** They give their employees the freedom to pursue their passions within the company and beyond the company.

- **They are unafraid to take risks.** They encourage calculated risk taking, relying heavily on facts and data to make choices. They test hypotheses and adjust course, when necessary, with relative ease.

- **They empower the team more than the individual manager.** Organizations that imbue managers with too much power tend to undermine the autonomy of individuals and the power of teams. These companies don't make that mistake. Granted, some may take autonomy too far—we're not yet believers in Zappos's "Holacracy" concept, which attempts to reshape managerial hierarchies completely. But it's possible for hierarchies and autonomous teams to coexist. Google, for instance, creates spans of control that are so broad that managers can't possibly micromanage the teams for which they are responsible.

- **Their cultures and business practices are guided by principles, not by rules.** Rules-driven cultures are only as good as the business logic built into the rules. In dynamic markets like those in which these companies must operate, it's virtually impossible to update and enact the rules with sufficient frequency. Principles-driven cultures, by contrast, are dynamic and are capable of adapting to new conditions in real time. These companies try to establish behavioral frameworks to guide ways of working, rather than creating a scorecard enforced by culture vigilantes.

Many will argue that it's easy for these high-flying companies, filled with young, ambitious employees, to build a people-centric, empowering, working environment. But any company can treat its workforce as an asset rather than as an expense. Think about the difference between the income statement and the balance sheet. When a company views "labor" as an item on the income statement—a cost—its focus will always be on minimizing the expense. When it views employees as a balance-sheet item—human capital, an asset— its goal will be to maximize the productive value of the asset. Plenty of companies give lip service to this distinction, but few have built a working environment that makes the most of the human capital on its balance sheet. Zeynep Ton, of MIT's Sloan School of Management, has written extensively about the power of the balance-sheet approach in her book *The Good Jobs Strategy*.[1] Examining the retail grocery industry, which includes many poorly paid service-sector jobs, she persuasively demonstrates how companies such as QuikTrip, Trader Joe's, Costco, and the Spanish grocer Mercadona have created superior business models founded on the twin ideas of operational excellence and treating employees as assets rather than as expenses.

The millennial high flyers and the more earthbound grocery retailers have all put into practice one critical belief: involve your people by treating them like adults, like people who seek meaning in their work, who are worthy of trust, and who are able to operate on their own without much oversight.

145

This is the kind of philosophy that lays the groundwork for inspiration and engagement.

Implementation: Follow the hierarchy of engagement practices. A company's philosophy on human motivation takes practical shape through many different elements. It's reflected in the value proposition a company offers its employees. It affects the operating model, the working environment, and modes of collaboration. Companies that take their philosophy seriously ensure that it addresses all the factors that determine employees' level of engagement and inspiration.

Before we examine these factors, there's one prerequisite, which is that an employee who feels he or she is in the wrong job will never be engaged or inspired, no matter how hard you try. So we assume before anything else that your company has an effective recruiting and placement system that matches people to jobs that suit them—simply put, one that enables your difference makers to make the biggest difference.

In our work, we find it useful to think about engagement as a spectrum ranging from satisfied to inspired and driven by a hierarchical model, which we call the pyramid of employee needs (see figure 6-2). At the lowest level are the qualifiers, which are necessary for a basic degree of satisfaction. Since you can't expect people to be engaged in their work unless their fundamental needs are met, these are the essentials. They include providing employees with a workplace that is safe, both physically and emotionally; providing the tools, training, and resources necessary to do a job well; ensuring that no one is obstructed by the organizational drag that comes with excess bureaucracy; and offering both fair monetary rewards and the feeling that the employee is valued. A

FIGURE 6-2

The pyramid of employee needs

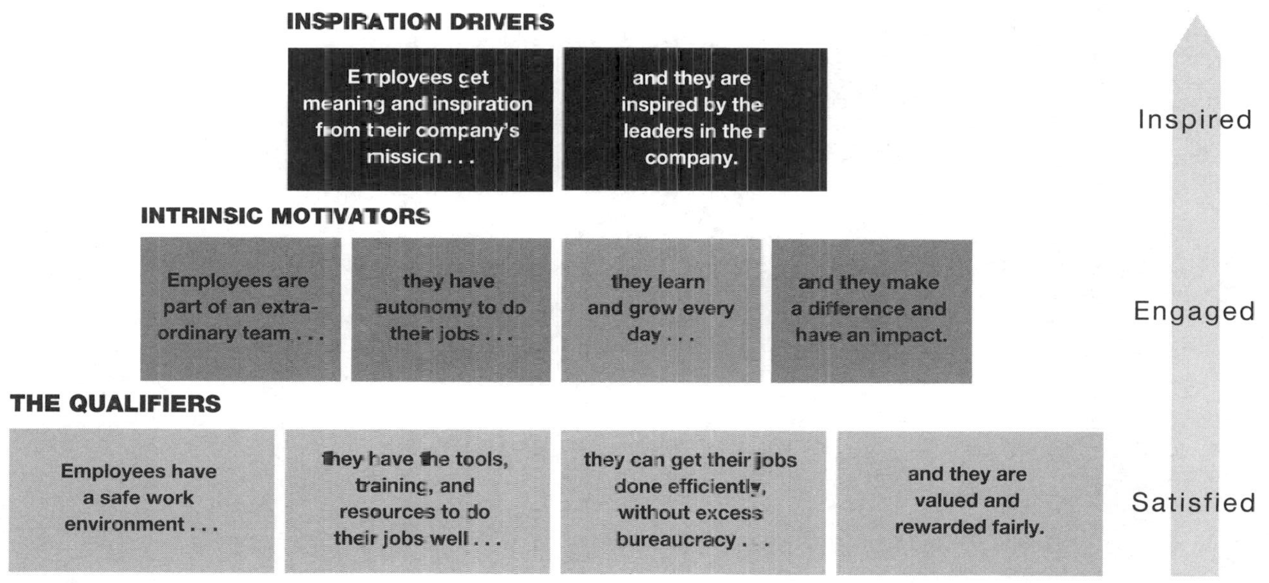

INSPIRATION DRIVERS

Employees get meaning and inspiration from their company's mission . . .

and they are inspired by the leaders in the company.

INTRINSIC MOTIVATORS

Employees are part of an extra-ordinary team . . .

they have autonomy to do their jobs . . .

they learn and grow every day . . .

and they make a difference and have an impact.

THE QUALIFIERS

Employees have a safe work environment . . .

they have the tools, training, and resources to do their jobs well . . .

they can get their jobs done efficiently, without excess bureaucracy . . .

and they are valued and rewarded fairly.

Inspired

Engaged

Satisfied

Source: Bain & Company

company that meets these needs will find that its employees are relatively content with their jobs and their work. They may not be fully engaged—and they may be open to leaving if a better opportunity crops up—but at least they are not backing their cars into parking spaces.

The next level in the pyramid includes the factors that begin to create deeper engagement. At this level, companies begin to unlock some of their employees' discretionary energy; they empower individuals and teams to take on extraordinary missions. The factors on this level are highly correlated with people's intrinsic motivations. In *Drive: The Surprising Truth About What Motivates Us*, Daniel Pink describes three key motivational elements: autonomy, mastery, and purpose.[2] A company that provides employees with appropriate levels of autonomy and the opportunity to achieve mastery of their work, both individually and as part of high-performing teams, will find that their productivity soars. Employees who achieve this level of engagement like the content of their jobs, enthusiastically show up for work every day, and will willingly take on new tasks and challenges.

The top layer of the pyramid adds the final dimension: inspiration. This is where engagement goes viral. Employees are not only individually inspired but also inspire others through their passion and their actions. People at this level become vocal advocates for the company. They believe in it, and they do extraordinary things to contribute to its success.

It's important to understand that these layers are sequential. The psychologist Abraham Maslow famously taught that human beings can't concern themselves with higher goals until their basic needs are met. The pyramid is a corporate analogue to Maslow's hierarchy. It reminds leaders that they can't expect employees to be engaged, let alone inspired, unless they have taken the steps necessary to ensure a safe, effective work environment with fair rewards. If they haven't, the very initiatives that are meant to foster engagement will feel like just one more energy-draining commitment—or like a cynical attempt to extract more hours out of an already stretched workforce. Attempts to inspire employees are particularly vulnerable to this sort of backfiring. Grandiose mission statements that are not anchored in the day-to-day reality of what the company does will ring false.

One consistent key to engagement, we have found, is to help individuals link their roles and individual missions to the company's purpose. This is especially compelling in service-intensive businesses; creating a connection between employees and the customers they serve turns the customer from a faceless abstraction into a real human being, and employees begin to see the link between their work and the company's mission. Nordstrom is one company that has done just this. In her article "The Path That Builds Trust," Jennifer Robin of the Great Place to Work Institute notes that Nordstrom has a single rule for employees: "Use good judgment in all situations." But it also establishes a single objective that is both clear and simple: "Our number one goal is to provide outstanding customer service." Setting this goal provides clarity to employees, as it "provides a guide for decision making, a standard for measurement, and also a philosophy about customer service that makes Nordstrom the industry leader they are." The company also provides employees with specific guidance as to the kind of behavior that is expected. In the words of one former employee, they include:

- A Nordstrom salesperson rarely points. If you have a question about where something is located, someone will walk you there.

- Salespeople are taught to walk your bagged purchase around the counter to you, versus just handing it across the counter.

- Salespeople can offer to ring up your purchase without you ever having to stand in line.

- Departments are generally trained to answer the phone on no more than the second ring.[3]

While each individual expectation is modest enough, they collectively shape a customer experience that few retailers can match.

To empower employees to act autonomously and in the best interest of customers, the company has designed an operating model and recognition system that are mutually reinforcing. For example, Nordstrom recognizes employees through an elite million-dollar club of top-performing employees. It empowers employees to act like small business owners, allowing them to "make use of their client list . . . to build and cultivate personal relationships with customers and take care of them as they see fit, or in other words operate their 'own' business within the larger company."[4] As a result, the company has become famous for nearly incredible stories of customer service. *Jacksonville Business Journal*, for instance, reported that a member of the housekeeping staff at a Nordstrom store in Connecticut discovered a customer's bags, along with her receipt and a flight itinerary, in the parking lot. Noticing that the customer had likely left directly from the store to catch her flight at Kennedy International Airport in New York, he looked up the customer's phone number in the company's system and tried to call her several times—*all while driving to the airport with her bags.* When she didn't answer her phone, the employee had the airport page her to let her know he had her bags.[5]

2. Balance employee autonomy with organizational needs

Central to any model of engagement and inspiration in modern, dynamic companies is the concept of employee autonomy; indeed, autonomy may be the single most important element in creating engagement or inspiration in any company. How can anyone feel engaged, let alone inspired, if she feels that some supervisor is always looking over her shoulder? But autonomy is a double-edged sword. On the one hand, it spurs creativity and involvement. On the other, unchecked autonomy can lead to ambiguity and inefficiencies, even organizational chaos. To find the right balance, you have to wrestle with three distinct challenges:

Balancing autonomy and accountability. An essential counterweight to autonomy is strict accountability for results, and for the actions and behaviors that deliver those results. In the words of a popular folk song from the 1960s, "freedom isn't free."

A company thus has to establish a strategy and purpose that provide context for employees' actions. It has to put the strategy into practice through measurable objectives, consistent measurement of progress toward those goals, feedback systems to monitor activities along the way, and appropriate consequences for reaching or failing to reach the goals. At their best, companies like those we mentioned realize that not everything is easily measurable or should be measured, and that constant temperature taking and micromanagement are both inefficient and demoralizing. But they also establish transparent boundary conditions and clear expectations. Employees and teams know they will be held accountable, and they know where the guardrails are. They understand the objectives, and they have a great deal of freedom in determining how to reach them within those guardrails. Clarity of purpose and what we call high-resolution strategies, which give people a clear view of where they're headed, provide the compass that can guide the choices teams and individuals make when working autonomously.

Balancing freedom to innovate versus following proven routines. All companies begin their lives as entrepreneurial ventures. As they grow, and as the industries they compete in mature, their leaders want to ensure that the organization gets the benefits of learning, and of the economies of scale that come from doing the same thing over and over. When this transition is managed well, companies create organizational mechanisms ensuring that best practices and proven routines are followed with rigor; they do this without creating too many rules and without draining the organization of its entrepreneurial energy. When it's managed poorly, companies create employees who follow the rulebooks to the point where they stop innovating.

The art and science here is determining how to get both outcomes—consistency and innovation—in the right proportion and in the appropriate parts of your organization. In many areas, freedom to innovate is the critical need. Think of new product development, or the parts of the company's value chain and business model that are undergoing significant reinvention because of digital transformations. In these activities, speed of innovation is critical, and the rallying cry should be autonomy, small teams, and organizational agility. Other areas, however, may benefit from standardized approaches. These are areas where consistent outcomes are essential and where speed of execution comes from deploying common methods, best practices, and enforced routines. The rallying cry here should be repeatability and efficiency. Each requires speed in different areas, innovation versus execution, and achieves these results in different ways. The challenge in striking the right balance is to know which method should predominate where, and how to design appropriate ways of working for each area. The wrong approach leads to confusion over goals and to ineffectiveness.

Balancing alignment with control. This task is closely related to the other two. In traditional hierarchical organizations, managers direct the work of subordinates and thereby ensure alignment with broader organizational goals. Spans of control are limited to a reasonable number—typically eight people or fewer—so that managers can effectively oversee their subordinates' efforts. This organizational model can work well in relatively stable business environments, where the pace of change is modest and where annual planning cycles suffice for managing strategic changes and course corrections. In more dynamic business environments, where innovation cycles happen in days or weeks rather than months and years, and where much of the work is cross-functional in nature and undertaken by small, agile teams, this type of organizational model can be slow to respond and innovate. Companies that take the approach of empowering autonomous teams must find ways to ensure coordination and connectivity among those teams without relying on controlling managers. Again, it's a matter of managerial art as well as science to achieve alignment without excessive control.

Spotify

It's helpful to look at a real-world example of a millennial company that has addressed these concerns.[6] Our favorite is the Swedish company Spotify. Spotify is a ten-year-old music, video, and podcast streaming company with 30 million paying subscribers and about $3 billion in revenue as of late summer 2016. Its two-thousand-plus employees are organized into agile teams, called squads, which are self-organizing, cross-functional, and colocated. Spotify has largely succeeded in maintaining an agile mindset and principles without sacrificing accountability. It enables innovation while keeping the benefits of repeatability, and it creates alignment without excessive control. Its lessons apply to many companies, not just digitally enabled service providers. Figure 6-3 shows the basic architecture of Spotify's organizational model.

Spotify's core organizational unit is an autonomous squad of no more than eight people. Each squad is accountable for a discrete aspect of the product, which it owns cradle to grave. Squads have the authority to decide what to build, how to build it, and with whom to work to make the product interoperable. They are organized into a light matrix called a tribe. Tribes comprise several squads linked together through a chapter, which is a horizontal grouping that helps to support specific competencies such as quality assistance, agile coaching, or web development. The chapter's primary role is to facilitate learning and competency development throughout the squads.

Leadership within the squad is self-determined, while the chapter leader is a formal manager, who focuses on coaching and mentoring. Spotify believes in the player-coach model: chapter leaders are also squad members. Squad members can switch squads and retain the same formal leader within their chapter. Spotify also introduced a third organizational element, known as a guild. Guilds are lightweight communities of interest whose primary purpose is to share knowledge in areas that cut across chapters and squads, such as leadership, continuous delivery, and web delivery.

FIGURE 6-3

The structure at Spotify

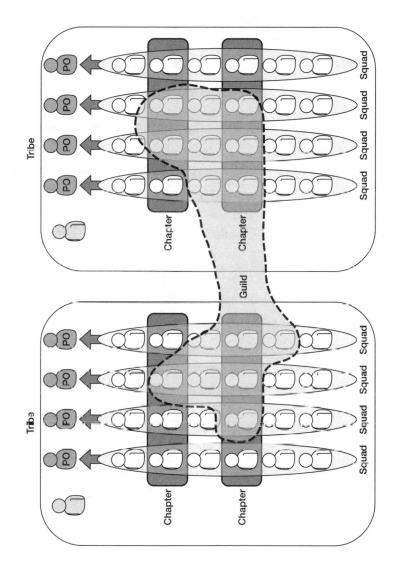

Source: Spotify.com

Note: "PO" in the figure stands for Product Owner.

This unusual combination of squads, tribes, chapters, and guilds is the organizational infrastructure that underlies Spotify's operating model. At first reading, it might sound like just another way to define a conventional organizational matrix in millennial, digital-friendly terms. But a closer examination reveals just how different the model really is and why it seems to work so well.

The squad structure achieves autonomy without sacrificing accountability. Every squad owns its features throughout the product's life cycle, and the squads have full visibility into their features' successes and failures. There is no single appointed leader of a squad; any such leadership role is emergent and informal. Results are visible both through internal reviews and through customer feedback, and squads are expected to fully understand successes and failures. Squads go through postmortem analyses of failures to ensure learning, and some squad rooms have "fail walls." Every few weeks, squads conduct retrospectives to evaluate what is going well and what needs to improve.

To ensure that the feedback process is effective for individuals as well as for the squads, Spotify redesigned its performance management system to separate salary discussion and performance evaluations from coaching and feedback. Before, peer feedback was incorporated into salary reviews; in Spotify's words, that "incentivized people to gather as many favorable reviews as possible rather than feedback around their biggest areas of potential improvement." Now, colleagues use an internal tool to invite anyone—including managers, peers, and direct reports—to provide feedback on results and on what an individual can do to improve. Employees may solicit feedback as often as they choose. In the words of Spotify employee Jonas Aman, "the result is a process that everyone needs to own and drive themselves, and it is about development and personal growth!"

Spotify encourages innovation without losing the benefits of repeatability. Since squads are the primary centers of innovation, Spotify introduced its chapters as the matrix to connect competencies across squads. Chapters in some ways are like a function-led center of expertise in a traditional model, which links center-led functions with business units. In Spotify's case, chapters have less formal authority, and they are organized around discrete competencies as opposed to broad functions. Guilds were added to facilitate experience sharing for horizontal topics of interest that are at a higher level than a specific competency. In the traditional model, central functions define and enforce standards and routinized processes from the top down. At Spotify, best-practice methods are discovered over time and determined by popular adoption from the bottom up. A practice or tool becomes a standard only when enough squads have adopted it and made it a de facto standard.

Culture—the subject of the following chapter—also plays a big role in keeping the innovation engine operating on all cylinders. Spotify has an experiment-friendly culture with an emphasis on test-and-learn approaches and contained experiments. If people don't know the best way to do something, they are likely to try alternative approaches and run several A/B tests to determine which is preferable. In place of opinion, ego, and authority, Spotify works hard to substitute data, experimentation, and open dialogue about root causes. It lowers the cost of failure through a decoupled architecture, so that a failure has a "limited blast radius" and affects only part of the user experience.

Spotify fosters alignment without excessive control. The central organizational feature that shapes Spotify's model is the concept of "loosely coupled, tightly aligned squads." The key belief here is that "alignment enables autonomy—the greater the alignment, the more autonomy you can grant." That's why the company spends so much time aligning on objectives and goals before launching into work. The leadership model at Spotify reinforces this alignment. A leader's job is to figure out the right problem and communicate it, so that squads can collaborate to find the best solution. Coordination comes through context and through a deep understanding of the company's priorities, product strategies, and overall mission. The release process decouples each element for feature squads, infrastructure squads, and client application squads. The ability to release features and then toggle them on or off enables full releases even before all features are fully operational. Here, too, the culture acts as a support. The watchword at Spotify is "be autonomous, but don't suboptimize—be a good citizen in the Spotify ecosystem." A common analogy at the company is a jazz band: each squad plays its instrument, but each also listens to the others and focuses on the overall piece to make great music.

Clearly, not all of Spotify's choices will be appropriate for every company; that's not the point. Rather, the point is that a company must make explicit choices in its operating model, ways of working, and culture that address the three core tensions between individual autonomy and organizational goals. Systematically aligning all elements of your operating model and working environment to create autonomy without sacrificing accountability, to get innovation where it matters most without sacrificing the benefits of scalability and repeatability, and to get alignment without excessive control are all at the heart of building an engaging and inspiring working environment.

3. Develop leaders who deliver results *and* inspire

Strong leadership is one of the most critical elements required to move from engagement to inspiration. In the Bain–Economist Intelligence Unit study, we asked respondents to rate their leadership team on their ability to inspire and motivate. The results are displayed in figure 6-4, and they are

FIGURE 6-4

Does your organization have leaders who inspire?

Please indicate the degree to which you agree with the following statements about leaders in your organization

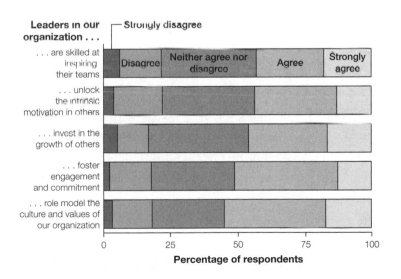

Source: Bain/EIU research (N = 308).

hardly encouraging. Barely half of the time did respondents "agree" or "strongly agree" that leaders were inspiring their people, or doing the things necessary to inspire.

One condition is clear: inspiration and performance must be inseparable. This is true both for strong leaders and for winning cultures. Who will be inspired by working for a company that turns in mediocre results? In observing hundreds of high-impact leaders across scores of companies worldwide, we consistently find that the strongest among them successfully drive both performance and inspiration. Leaders who deliver only performance may do so at a cost that the organization is unwilling to bear. Those who focus only on inspiration may find that they motivate the troops only to be undermined by mediocre outcomes. Given the outsized impact leaders have on shaping cultures, it should not be surprising that we believe both should be evaluated by the strength of their performance orientation *and* their ability to inspire.

Effective leadership isn't generic. To achieve great performance, companies need a common leadership profile that reflects their unique strategy, business model, and culture—in other words, a common behavioral signature, as described in chapter 4. Just as a company must "spike" in certain capability areas to create competitive advantage, leaders must have behavioral spikes that are relevant to their company's model of value creation. The winning behavioral signature is unique to a company but should be common across the leaders within the company. Achieving inspiration, however, requires a different approach. Our experience has shown us time and again that every leader has the potential to be inspirational by drawing on his or her unique strengths. The combination of attributes that lead to inspirational leadership are thus unique to the individual.

Developing inspirational leaders. There are few rigorous methods to measure someone's ability to inspire, to systematically develop that intangible quality, or to embed those skills throughout an organization. "Leadership as an area of intellectual inquiry remains thin, and little original thought has been given to what leader learning in the second decade of the twenty-first century should look like," observes Barbara Kellerman of Harvard Kennedy School.

To understand what enables a leader to be inspirational, we and our colleagues conducted extensive primary research. Starting with an initial survey of two thousand employees, we asked respondents to rate how inspired they were by their colleagues. We also asked them to rate what was important in contributing to that sense of inspiration. While inspiration may seem difficult to decipher, we identified thirty three distinct and tangible attributes, depicted in figure 6-5, that are statistically significant in creating inspiration in others. We built this list from multiple disciplines, including psychology, neurology, sociology, organizational behavior, and management science, as well as from extensive interviews.

We then grouped the characteristics that inspire in four quadrants that highlight the setting in which they tend to work their magic. One quadrant, for example, contains the qualities related to leading a team, such as focus, harmony, and direction. Another quadrant, including stress tolerance, optimism, and emotional self-awareness, comprises behaviors that develop one's inner resources. While these quadrants provide a structure that makes the model easier to digest, they do not emphasize any particular distribution of abilities. Our research demonstrates that each of the elements is important to the collective inspirational health of an organization, and that no particular combination is more

FIGURE 6-5

Bain inspirational leadership model

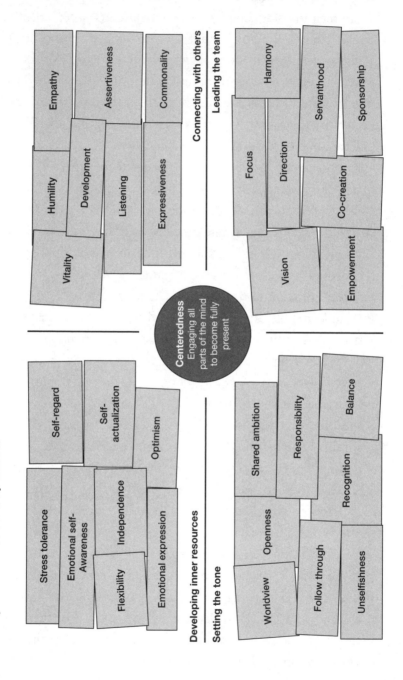

powerful than others in contributing to an individual's capacity to inspire.

Next we assessed people's ability to inspire. We defined an individual's distinguishing strengths as those ranking within the top 10 percent of one's peer group. We labeled the characteristics ranked between the seventieth and ninetieth percentiles "potential distinguishing strengths," and those in the bottom 10 percent "weaknesses." The remaining 60 percent of the ranking are neutral characteristics, because one's level of skill neither detracts from nor contributes to a differential effect on others. The results of our research revealed four critical insights into building effective coaching programs to help your leaders raise their inspiration quotient:

- Having even one distinguishing strength—that is, ranking in the top 10 percent of your peer group on one of those characteristics—nearly doubles your chances of being a leader who inspires others.

- The more distinguishing strengths you have, the more inspirational you can be. Having just four of those attributes as distinguishing strengths is sufficient to make someone highly inspiring. More than 90 percent of those demonstrating distinguishing strengths on four or more of the thirty-three elements are inspirational to their colleagues.

- People who inspire are incredibly diverse. Any combination of distinguishing strengths works; there is no fixed archetype of an inspirational leader. This finding underscores the power of authenticity. Inspirational leaders come in many varieties.

- Everyone has the ability to become inspiring by focusing on his or her strengths as opposed to fixing weaknesses. This is consistent with a growing body of research. According to Gallup, for example, the odds of employees being engaged are 73 percent when an organization's leadership focuses on the strengths of its employees, compared to 9 percent when they do not.

A surprising result of the research was that *centeredness* turned out to be the single most important attribute among the thirty-three. It was the most statistically significant in creating inspiration, and it was the trait that employees most want to develop. Centeredness is a state of greater mindfulness, achieved by engaging every part of the mind. While a growing number of companies offer optional mindfulness programs to promote health and workplace satisfaction, our research shows that centeredness is fundamental to the ability to lead. It improves one's ability to stay level-headed, cope with stress, empathize with others, and listen more deeply.

Right now, leading companies are beginning to develop programs based on these principles. They understand that their competitive edge depends on their ability to deliver a great customer experience. They know that the nature of work has changed, and that today's employees are looking for more from their jobs than a paycheck and a pat on the back. They also know that talented people have lots of opportunities and must be re-recruited all the time. So these companies seek out and value the leaders who truly inspire people, and they proactively develop those inspirational skills throughout their organization. Conventional leadership development programs might have been sufficient in a twentieth-century enterprise. But today's world is different—faster moving, more demanding, and more open. Inspirational skills, properly supported and developed, are one key to a more productive future—and to a workplace where people don't back their cars into the parking lot.

The more employees a company can effectively engage and inspire, the higher the organization's productive power. People who devote more of their individual discretionary energy to the company's success are more productive and make those around them more productive. But employee engagement requires more than colorful posters in the headquarters lobby, free gourmet coffee in the cafeteria, or volleyball over lunch. It requires careful management—from the top—and dedication to creating an environment where people will bring more of their whole selves to work. Also, as we've argued throughout this chapter, pursuing engagement alone is aiming too low. The best-performing companies manage to inspire a large percentage of their workforce. They expect their leaders to deliver both performance and inspiration. All this enables these companies to make the utmost of their human capital.

FOUR WAYS TO BUILD INSPIRATION AND ENGAGEMENT

1. *Help employees build greater connection* between their daily work and the company's customer or social mission. Ask whether you are running a company where employees want to "back in or head in" in the morning.

2. *Develop a humane philosophy and implement it.* Translate it into an employee value proposition, operating model,

working environment, and ways of working that address the entire set of engagement drivers. Determine the right degree of emphasis for each element based on your strategy, business model, and culture.

3. *Create a high-autonomy organization without losing the benefits of scalability and repeatability.* Strike the optimal balance between autonomy and organizational needs. Ask whether you have actively eliminated needless bureaucracy, micromanaging, and overly prescriptive rule books.

4. *Invest in inspirational leadership development.* That's how you create leaders who are skilled both at delivering exceptional results and inspiring employees.

7

Build a Winning Culture

This book has offered a lot of prescriptions for overcoming organizational drag, attracting and deploying great talent, and unleashing the energy and enthusiasm that people bring to their work. We've argued for freeing up time and eliminating unnecessary bureaucracy. We've discussed simplifying the organization, and we've emphasized finding and deploying the people who really make a difference. We've provided a pragmatic model for attracting, engaging, and inspiring your employees to do amazing things.

These prescriptions usually provoke two frustratingly simple and deceptive questions:

All this seems pretty much like common sense. Why doesn't it happen in the ordinary course of business?

If we follow these prescriptions, how do we make sure that they all stick—and that we get and sustain the results we're looking for?

The answer to both questions comes down to a clichéd but critical element of any organization: its culture. On the first question: many companies don't take these seemingly commonsensical steps because they don't fit with the company's culture. Try to implement them and the culture attacks them like an immune system ridding the body of a foreign intruder. On the second: culture will determine whether the changes you make can last, and whether they will generate the results you seek. Get the cultural elements right and your other steps will fall into place, even reinforce one another. Get culture wrong and you'll find yourself constantly frustrated, because nothing will stick. Former IBM CEO Lou Gerstner captured it well when he said, "Until I came to IBM, I probably would have told you that culture was just one among several important elements in any organization's makeup and success . . . I came to see, in my time at IBM, that culture isn't just one aspect of the game; it is the game."[1]

He's not alone. A winning culture is at the heart of virtually every sustainably successful company. It is probably the single most enduring source of competitive advantage. Such a culture is your greatest defense against stagnation and creeping complexity. It allows you to punch above your weight by creating virtual scale through collaboration and engaged employees. Strong cultures are also talent magnets. In research we conducted in 2013, we compared the strength of a company's culture with employees' eagerness to recommend it to a friend. The measure we used was an employee Net Promoter Score. We asked individuals, "On a zero-to-ten scale, how likely are you to recommend your company as a place to work to a close friend?" A score of ten meant very likely, zero not at all likely. In keeping with Net Promoter System terminology, we characterized those scoring nine or ten as promoters and those scoring six or less as detractors. The employee Net Promoter Score is the difference between the percentage of promoters and the percentage of detractors. Using this measure, companies with strong cultures scored more than 74 percent on our scale; those with weak ones scored less than 62 percent.

Similar research by Futurestep, a division of Korn Ferry, found that nearly two-thirds of the one thousand executives surveyed believe that cultural reputation is the single most important recruiting advantage for global organizations.[2] A strong culture, like deep engagement and inspiration, essentially re-recruits your difference makers every day; it means that you don't have to constantly entice them with special incentives to stay. In our index of productivity, culture's role is to help concentrate organizational energy on the high-performance behaviors that are most critical to your strategy.

Since culture has been so widely discussed, many of the executives we talk to are a little sick of hearing about it. "We're not Southwest Airlines," they tell us, a hint of exasperation in their voices. "We're not Google, and we're not some hot startup. We're a century-old company in an everyday business, with ways of doing things that haven't changed much in decades. How are we supposed to redo our culture?" The question is compelling, and we'll try to answer it in this chapter. We'll unpack the building blocks of culture. We'll look in some detail at everyday companies that *have* rebuilt and regenerated a winning culture, and at the three critical measures they have taken to do so. Our hope is that you will see culture as the keystone in the arch of what we're proposing—and that the arch won't collapse because it lacks that critical keystone. For all these reasons, culture needs to be on the top of the CEO's agenda.

The building blocks of culture

Of course, "putting culture on the agenda" is easy to say and hard to do. Culture is a complex amalgam of social elements. It comprises all of the intangible forces that influence what people do and what they believe, how they act and interact. In a well-known formulation, it determines how people behave when no one is looking. Culture may be reflected in lists of values or in mission statements, but it isn't defined by them. Nor is it the same as strategy or operating model. Strategy focuses employees on specific outcomes and on the activities necessary to achieve those outcomes. An operating model creates the environment within which work is done; it facilitates (or obstructs) individual and collective accomplishment. Culture infuses them both with the human elements of beliefs, purposes, and values. It directs people's energy and shapes how they act and interact, individually and collectively, to achieve the desired outcomes.

Cultures are shaped both by what we call the internal compass and by the organizational environment. (Figure 7-1 represents this graphically.) The internal compass comprises a meaningful purpose, winning values, and reinforcing beliefs. In strong cultures, the organizational environment reinforces the internal compass. Organizational environment is a deliberately broad concept: it includes leaders' actions role-modeling the desired behaviors, a consequence-based reinforcement system to reward those behaviors, and an operating model and talent system that find, develop, and promote the right people and enable them to do the right things. Let's look at each of these elements in a little more depth.

FIGURE 7-1

Anatomy of a winning culture

A system of shared purpose, values, beliefs, and behaviors that drive superior engagement and performance.

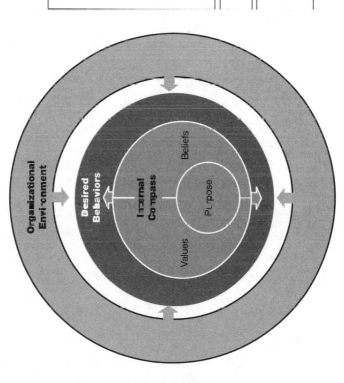

- **Internal compass:** nonnegotiables that guide behaviors and decisions
  - Meaningful purpose: A shared customer or socially centered purpose that employees find meaningful and proud to be a part of
  - Winning values: core attributes that are hallmarks of winning organizations
    ▸ Accountability, collaboration, agility, innovation, ambition, integrity, people-orientation
  - Reinforcing beliefs: unique to company based on industry context, strategic choices and company heritage

- **Desired behaviors:** Daily behaviors that connect purpose, values and beliefs

- **Organizational environment:** Operating model, talent systems, rewards and consequences, and leadership actions that influence ways of working and behaviors

Source: Bain & Company

Purpose. A winning culture begins with a meaningful purpose that the company can translate into individual roles and missions. The purpose is most powerful when it is defined in terms of an ambitious customer or social mission. Some of our favorites include:

- Starbucks—"To inspire and nurture the human spirit— One Person, One Cup and One Neighborhood at a time."

- Mahindra—"We will challenge conventional thinking and innovatively use all of our resources to drive positive change in the lives of our stakeholders and communities across the world to enable them to Rise."

- Facebook—"Give people the power to share and make the world more open and connected."

- Ikea—"Our vision is to create a better everyday life for the many people. Our business idea supports this vision by offering a wide range of well-designed, functional home furnishing products at prices so low that as many people as possible will be able to afford them."

Values and beliefs. A company's purpose rests on a set of values and on beliefs that reflect these values. In another 2013 study, we tested the importance of nearly twenty distinct values in creating a winning culture. Seven stood out from the pack: *innovation*, including the courage to take informed risks and learn from mistakes; *ambitions*, openly seeking and embracing stretch missions; *high integrity*, with honest communications and a respect for the highest ethical standards; *accountability*, with a bias toward what is best for the company rather than best for the individual; *collaboration*, displaying mutual trust and teamwork; *agility*, expecting and anticipating change; and a *people orientation*, focused on building human relationships by connecting employees to the company's mission through a rewarding and engaging work environment, connecting the C-suite to the front line to engage and inspire, and connecting both to the customer and community to reinforce the company's purpose. We find these values to be universally present in winning cultures.

Reinforcing beliefs have an equally important role to play in creating high-performance behaviors. Unlike values, which are universal, beliefs are a unique articulation of identity and priorities based on things like a company's heritage, place of origin, social context, or founder's imprint. The company's purpose, the seven universal values, and the reinforcing beliefs collectively shape the belief system of the organization—its North Star, so to speak. But the belief system alone isn't enough to create a winning culture. It must then be translated into a company-specific set of behaviors. That is where culture comes to life, and where it provides power to the organization.

Behaviors. Behavior is where the rubber meets the road. Many companies have business practices and ways of working that are at odds with their stated purpose and values. In this group, cultural forces act like the antibodies we described earlier, rejecting any attempts at change. Other companies bring their purpose and values to life every day through the way they work. Here the effect is the opposite: cultural forces suppress behaviors that contradict the espoused purpose and values. Behaviors come to life and are reinforced both in big, symbolic moments of truth, when all eyes are on leaders as they make major decisions, and in the smaller, more routine moments of truth that characterize daily decisions and interactions.

As we discussed in the previous chapter, the most effective leaders accomplish two objectives: they drive performance and they inspire others. A strong culture has a similar effect, in that it fosters both performance and engagement. Companies that engage employees' hearts and minds unlock their intrinsic motivations and discretionary energy, fueling agility, speed, and performance. Cultures that drive performance attract individuals who want to make a difference. An environment filled with committed colleagues, like a team with players committed to winning, is inspiring and engaging.

Many companies try to initiate a cultural transformation whenever they reinvent their business model. Some work hard to instill a performance orientation. Others focus on building engagement through a better working environment and employee value proposition. These two endeavors often end up as separate tracks of work. For example, a company might attempt to boost accountability as part of strengthening its performance orientation. It might translate its business goals into individual objectives and establish specific outcome-based metrics and incentives. It might even install a new management dashboard and a related monthly operations review process to measure these key performance indicators. All that can be very powerful, but if you do it without also empowering teams and individuals to achieve their objectives, you can end up micromanaging and micromeasuring outcomes, thus destroying the very engagement and accountability you are trying to create. To succeed, cultural renewal has to address both components simultaneously, linking the performance and engagement interventions so that they reinforce rather than contradict one another.

Let's bring this rather abstract discussion of culture to life with an example.

Restoring a high-performance culture: the case of AB InBev

We promised at the beginning of this chapter that we would discuss everyday companies—the established incumbents of the corporate world—not just the upstarts and acknowledged culture heroes. We did so because we believe it is possible for incumbent companies to be every bit as dynamic, as high performing, and as involving for employees as the founder-led upstarts. If you don't believe that, consider the story of the company now known as Anheuser-Busch InBev (AB InBev).

AB InBev traces its roots to a tiny beer company in Brazil, originally known as Companhia Cervejaria Brahma, which was bought by the 3G Capital founders in the late 1980s for about $60 million. That company was successful, and it expanded throughout Brazil and South America, eventually emerging as AmBev after a merger with Antarctica in 1999. AmBev then merged with Interbrew, a Belgium-based brewer, and the combination later bought out Anheuser-Busch, at that point the biggest beer company in the United States. The 2016 combination of AB InBev and SAB Miller united two of the top five global players in the industry.

Brewing is an old, mature industry, and many of the companies that make up AB InBev were founded centuries ago. Our colleagues Chris Zook and James Allen have written extensively about the power of a "founder's mentality" as an animating force within great companies and as an owner's repair manual to help companies that have lost their entrepreneurial energy.[3] In some sense, AB InBev has had two sets of founders: the original founders and the new founders, who acquired these companies. In most cases, the spirit of the original founders was long gone. But the new founders have instilled an ownership-infused, performance-oriented culture into the large companies they acquired. In the process, they created an enterprise that inspires its employees to achieve remarkable results.[4]

AB InBev describes three factors at the heart of its model: dream, people, and culture.

Dream big and set a bold ambition. AB InBev calls its ambition the "dream." As CEO Carlos Brito is fond of saying, "dreaming big or small takes the same amount of energy, so why not dream big?" AB InBev says its dream is to be the best beer company "bringing people together for a better world." Being the best means that no one can afford to be complacent. AB InBev typically sets an ambition, makes progress toward achieving it, and then sets a new one—"opening and closing the gap," in company language. It applies this process at every level of the organization.

Simplify the operating model. This is where "people" come in. When 3G or AB InBev acquires a company, one of the first actions executives take is to examine the acquired entity's organizational structure and operating model. They immediately eliminate duplicate responsibilities and eradicate any ambiguities in accountabilities. AB InBev aspires to build an organization with no more than five layers and with fixed spans of control dictated by a clear blueprint. This significant delayering of the organization collapses the distance between the leadership team and the front line. It helps the company spend its dollars wisely, and it reinforces a culture where everyone is a "doer" rather than an overseer. AB InBev establishes a leadership profile—a behavioral signature—that indicates the kind of people it is looking for: hungry to make a difference, frugal, never satisfied, results focused, hard working, data-driven, deeply connected to the front line and to customers with a deep, pragmatic knowledge of their business area or discipline.

Embed ownership values into ways of working. The sidebar "AB InBev's 10 Principles" shows the ten principles that inform AB InBev's approach; seven of the ten are devoted to culture. Just as in our model of a winning culture—behaviors informed by universal values and company-specific beliefs—AB InBev's principles contain a mix. Some are universal values, such as accountability (principle #6) and integrity (principle #10). Others articulate highly specific beliefs that are deeply rooted in the company, such as a strong bias against unnecessary complexity and costs as captured in principles #7 and #8. Many people who work at AB InBev make a point of saying that these are not just words on a page; they inform everything the company does and are deeply embedded in its ways of working. Some examples will illustrate.

When InBev merged with Anheuser-Busch in 2008, Anheuser's headquarters were in a large low-rise building in St. Louis,

AB InBev's 10 Principles

DREAM

1. Our shared dream energizes everyone to work in the same direction to be the *Best Beer Company Bringing People Together for a Better World.*

PEOPLE

2. Our greatest strength is our people. Great *People* grow at the pace of their talent and are *rewarded* accordingly.

3. We recruit, develop, and retain people who can be *better* than ourselves. We will be judged by the *quality* of our teams.

CULTURE

4. We are *never completely satisfied* with our results, which are the fuel of our company. Focus and *zero-complacency* guarantee a lasting advantage.

5. The consumer is the *Boss*. We serve our consumers by offering brand experiences that play a meaningful role in their lives, and always in a responsible way.

6. We are a company of *owners*. Owners take *results personally*.

7. We believe *common sense* and *simplicity* are usually better guidelines than unnecessary sophistication and complexity.

8. We manage our costs tightly, to free up resources that will support sustainable and profitable *top line growth*.

9. Leadership by personal example is at the core of our culture. *We do what we say.*

10. *We never take shortcuts. Integrity, hard work, quality, and responsibility* are key to building our company.

Source: "10 Principles," AB InBev, http://www.ab-inbev.com/about/dream-people-culture.html.

Missouri. The top floor housed the office of the CEO and a few of his direct reports. The furnishings were elegant, with turn-of-the-century oil paintings and a grand boardroom. Four massive corner offices, each with a private bathroom, were surrounded by desks for the executives' assistants.

AB InBev's culture values openness and abhors the trappings of hierarchy, so one of the first moves the company made was to demolish the top-floor space and create an open-floor plan. All this took place in 2008, at the height of the financial crisis, when InBev had just paid $52 billion for Anheuser-Busch and had taken on billions of dollars in debt to finance the deal. Even though budgets were tight, the symbolic and cultural importance of opening up the space was worth far more than the modest amount of money required to remodel it. And that wasn't the only example of taking quick action to restore an ownership mindset. For instance, Anheuser-Busch had a small fleet of planes and more than a dozen pilots on staff. The decision to sell the planes and furlough the pilots was easy.

While these symbolic actions sent strong messages to employees about AB InBev's values, the most powerful changes have come in the form of new ways of working. Anheuser-Busch's dress code went out the window; jeans came in. (Brito says, "Our customers don't wear suits and ties, so why should we?") Brito and his leadership team work around a shared table, lowering the barriers to informal, one-on-one discussion and decision making. As we noted earlier, people have easy access to the data they need for decisions; the culture encourages face-to-face communications and meetings structured for discussion rather than for presentations.

The idea of spending every company dollar like your own comes to life in the routines and rituals surrounding AB

InBev's much-discussed zero-based budgeting (ZBB) process. World-class cost management systems create highly detailed views of costs and cost drivers. Managers armed with this information and with AB InBev's bold ambitions scrutinize the data, figuring out how to do more with less. In truth, however, the power of this process depends only partly on the tools that are used; other companies have attempted to implement ZBB and typically struggle to get even half the benefit. (Recently, another consumer packaged goods company announced that it, too, was adopting ZBB; a skeptical analyst who examined its targets quipped that it felt more like "1G.") The reasons are cultural: most companies don't have the appetite for the disruption that is required, and they lack both the ambitious dream and the "opening and closing the gap" mindset. Nor do they embrace the daily, weekly, and monthly routines and rituals that bring discipline to cost management, or link their cost ambitions to an objective performance-management and incentive system.

Interventions to reactivate a performance culture

AB InBev is hardly alone in transforming the culture of a once-stodgy business. Alan Mulally reshaped the culture of Ford Motor Company and effected a remarkable turnaround. Peter Coleman led a revival of Woodside, the Australian oil and gas company. Howard Schultz returned to Starbucks, the company he had founded, and brought that iconic company's culture back to life. When you look closely at such experiences, you find that they all involve the three sorts of interventions captured in figure 7-2. The new leaders raise

FIGURE 7-2

Three interventions to activate a performance culture

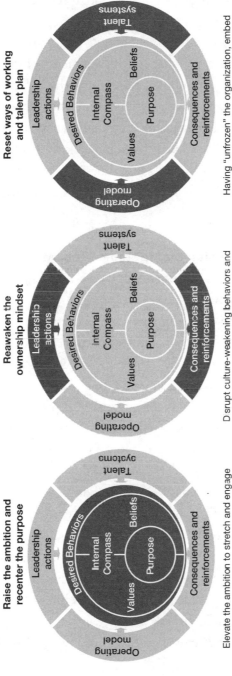

Raise the ambition and recenter the purpose

Elevate the ambition to stretch and engage the organization. Reenergize and recenter your purpose by linking each individual's role to the company's customer mission

<u>Litmus test:</u> Can you see your company's purpose come to life every day in your employees' actions?

Reawaken the ownership mindset

Disrupt culture-weakening behaviors and routines through leadership role-modeling at critical moments of truth and a consistent consequence-based reinforcement system

<u>Litmus test:</u> Have you created a culture of renters or owners?

Reset ways of working and talent plan

Having "unfrozen" the organization, embed the high-performance behaviors in your operating model, better ways of working, and talent management systems

<u>Litmus test:</u> Are you encouraging and embedding culture-strengthening or culture-weakening behaviors?

Source: Bain & Company

the company's strategic ambitions and recenter its purpose in a bold customer or social mission. They reawaken the ownership mindset and an orientation to performance through "constructive disruptions" at specific moments of truth, both the symbolic and the routine, reinforcing the behaviors they want to see with feedback systems and with consequence-based performance-management systems. They also reset the company's operating model, especially its ways of working, to embed the change, at the same time renewing their talent-management systems to attract difference makers and engage the workforce.

Intervention 1: Raise the strategic ambition and recenter the company's purpose. In Bain's 2013 study of cultural transformations, survey respondents said the single most important act a company can undertake to galvanize change is creating a bold ambition and compelling vision. That means defining the purpose, values, and behaviors that shape how people work and that provide context for the mission of individuals and teams. The process normally starts with the senior leadership team, but it also requires a thoughtful plan for engaging and enrolling the rest of the organization.

This is essentially what Kent Thiry had to do when he took the reins of DaVita, the kidney-dialysis company we mentioned in the prologue. At that time—it was 1999—the company was known as Total Renal Care. It had expanded rapidly during the previous decade, including an acquisition of Renal Treatment Centers valued at more than a billion dollars, but it was now in serious trouble. It had "460 [treatment] centers doing things 460 different ways," according to one observer.

Patient outcomes were poor relative to industry standards, and employee turnover was high. Shareholders had mounted a lawsuit against the company; the government was investigating its practices; and it was losing more than $60 million a year. "Total Renal Care was a disaster of a company," wrote a Bank of America analyst. "All they did was buy things instead of focus on running the company."

Thiry and his mostly new management team took quick action to stabilize the business, including addressing the lawsuit, the investigation, and the continuing losses. But then he began the cultural turnaround. He flew seven hundred leaders to Phoenix to talk about the company's mission and values. He engaged the entire population of employees in a seven-month exercise to choose its new name. (DaVita derives from an Italian phrase meaning "he who gives life.") He completely raised the company strategic ambition and reset its purpose. "Our vision for DaVita was to be more than just a dialysis company," he wrote. "It was to be a community that just happens to be organized in the form of a company. DaVita does dialysis, but is not about dialysis. DaVita is about life . . . When we succeed in creating a special working environment for our teammates, they in turn create a special clinical and caring environment for our patients and their families." Over time, he led the creation of a company that is inspiring in its commitment to patients, transparent and highly democratic in its operations, and a magnet for talented people who want to work in health care. Employee retention has improved dramatically. Patient outcomes are significantly better than before, and better than those of DaVita's competitors. Financially, the company has created billions of dollars in value for shareholders since Thiry's arrival.

Intervention 2: Reawaken the ownership mindset. Once you have defined or redefined the purpose, values, and behaviors you want to see, you need to pick a handful of the most important behavior changes and concentrate on embedding them. This often requires purposeful and constructive disruption of established behaviors and culture-weakening routines, and it typically involves two key activities: identifying the leadership actions and triggers that precede the desired behavior, and designing a robust set of consequences (positive and negative) to send reinforcing or correcting signals. The most successful leaders focus on moments of truth—those times when an employee must make a critical decision about how to behave—and pick only one or two of the most important elements to change. Three quick vignettes will help demonstrate what we mean.

- When Paul O'Neill became CEO of Alcoa in 1987, he knew that he needed to focus the company on workplace safety. To show his commitment to the goal, he required that he be notified of all safety incidents within twenty-four hours. Safety improved dramatically, to the point where Alcoa's worker injury rate fell to 25 percent of the US average.

- When Howard Schultz returned to Starbucks as CEO after a nearly eight-year hiatus, he realized that Starbucks's unique customer-focused coffee experience was now in the backseat. In the front seat were automation and diversification, both implemented in pursuit of throughput and growth. Schultz took swift action to change the company's direction; he even shut down 7,100 US stores for three hours on February 26, 2008, to retrain the baristas in the art of making espresso. In this highly symbolic move, he left no doubt about his intentions—and about what he thought it would take to make Starbucks great again.

- When Alan Mulally came to Ford in 2006 to help turn around the business, he took bold actions to change the way the company operated. In one highly visible moment, he applauded Mark Fields (who would eventually become his successor) for admitting to a failure in an executive meeting. That was pretty much unheard of at Ford, and it set the tone for the open and honest communications required for a new culture at the company.

Cultural change often involves leadership change, as in all three of the vignettes. Many activist investors subscribe to the belief that the best formula for managing change is to change management. Further, employees are often reluctant to embrace cultural renewal programs if they believe that the organization will eventually return to the same old culture-weakening patterns because nothing has changed at the top of the house. In our experience, cultural transformations can be effected without complete leadership swap-outs, but they require more sustained effort.

Whether or not there is a change of leadership, an organization trying to change must address culture-strengthening and culture-weakening routines and behaviors. Broad, diffuse efforts are doomed to failure. Let's go back and look at the seven universal values we listed as part of a high-performance culture, and at the specific actions a company might take at moments of truth to strengthen or weaken them (see table 7-1).

One powerful idea for reawakening a mature company's entrepreneurial spirit and energy emerged from research our

TABLE 7-1

Seven universal values

	Culture strengthening	Culture weakening
Innovation	• Recognize and celebrate risk taking when it was done on a data-driven basis, even if the outcome was not as expected. • Create time and space to explore ideas in an unconstrained manner.	• Firing someone for bad outcomes related to informed risk taking. • Constraining resources and time to the point that little effort is focused on thinking boldly and from the future back.
Ambition	• Setting targets that are stretching without 100% certainty they can be achieved.	• Setting targets in annual plans and performance contracts that are achievable to ensure consistent payout of bonuses for fear of demotivating employees.
High integrity	• 100% adherence to established ethical standards. • Surfacing and debating ideas in public forums with complete follow-through by all participants, even those with dissenting views, once the path is chosen.	• Overlooking minor ethical lapses or keeping high performers who violate cultural norms. • Allowing pocket vetoes by executives or passive noncompliance with the plan.
Accountability	• Strong commitment to designing in the right mix of autonomy and accountability. • Building an operating model and ways of working that allow for agility but not ambiguity on accountabilities. • Committed to a recognition and rewards system that celebrates results, not promises or intentions.	• Embracing management practices that are overly directive, overmeasured, and micromanaged. • Leaving excessive accountability ambiguity in the model and expecting teamwork and collaboration alone to resolve. • Egalitarian recognition and rewards systems.

Collaboration	• Empowering teams of high-performing individuals. • Embracing diversity and constructive tensions to ensure the best ideas come forward and are fully considered. • Externally focused with influence gained through building partnerships and collaborations. • Design in structures, processes, and forums to create appropriate levels of constructive tension, while also developing ways of working to quickly resolve these tensions.	• Empowering managers and hierarchies. • Allowing the loudest or most senior voices to dominate discussions. Failing to create methods of resolving tensions constructively and quickly. • Internally focused with influence gained through managing internal politics. • Valuing consensus over constructive tension.
Agility	• Systematically eliminating strategic, organizational, and process complexity that dilutes accountability and impedes speed. • Investing in making change a core competency and realizing that change only happens with leadership, sponsorship, and effort. • Embracing agile principles and ways of working and knowing when to drive repeatable routines or innovate new ways of working.	• Allowing complexity and bureaucracy to perpetuate ways of working that rob the organization of time, talent, and energy. • Expecting change to happen once decisions are made and plans established. • Expecting playbooks, standards, heuristics, and rules to direct individual actions and behaviors.
People orientation	• Building an operating model and talent system that emphasize performance and engagement in mutually reinforcing ways. • Anchoring the company's purpose in an inspiring customer-centered mission.	• Creating a working environment that sacrifices performance for engagement or engagement for performance. • Creating a purpose that lacks credibility and is far removed from the content of an employee's daily life.

colleagues Chris Zook and James Allen undertook for their book *The Founder's Mentality*. They label the idea a "micro battle." A micro battle is a carefully defined competitive arena, typically at the intersection of a specific customer segment in a specific geographic region, and involving a specific set of competitors. Such battles lie at the heart of a company's repeatable model for value creation; winning them is critical to defending a company's core areas and to opening up new ones. The genius of the idea is not so much in identifying micro battles as in fighting them: companies typically unleash several entrepreneurial cross-functional teams to execute missions in a series of fast, sharp, closed-loop efforts. Such moves boost the company's heart rate and get the organizational blood flowing. They also can develop internal entrepreneurs who act as catalysts to help the company reawaken its insurgent mission.

Intervention 3: Reset ways of working and talent plan. It's not enough just to disrupt normal routines. As the saying goes, organizations don't change, people change. In other words, people have to modify how they behave, and changing behaviors is hard work. Most of us even have trouble altering our own behavior and sustaining the change—witness the fact that health clubs are crowded in early January and empty by late February. An organization that asks its people to change will run into the same obstacles and will have to reinforce the message over and over again.

Systematically working through each element of your operating model and talent system with an eye toward bolstering culture-strengthening attributes and eliminating culture-weakening attributes is a powerful way of ensuring that the actions you take will actually drive engagement and inspiration.

The list of actions is likely to include powerful steps like the following:

- **Don't let the matrix obscure accountability.** Make sure every business outcome is owned by a single individual or team with the resources, accountability, and authority to deliver the planned result.

- **Collapse the distance from the C-suite to the front line.** The secret here is radical delayering, which empowers everyone in the chain of command to take more responsibility.

- **Tear down the walls.** Change the physical work environment to create more intimate workspaces. Lower the barriers to collaboration; connect senior management more directly to the rest of the organization.

- **Get face-to-face when it is necessary.** Too much remote work or too many virtual meetings leads to loss of connectivity and a weakening of the culture over time.

- **Discussions, not presentations.** Stop for a moment and look at the last PowerPoint presentation you received. People often number their decks to maintain version control. What version is it on now? (Our guess is double digits.) How many thousands of person hours were spent building this presentation—and was it worth it? Discussion with informed individuals who are close to the customer and the front line is usually more valuable than any number of PowerPoint slides.

- **"I don't know" is OK.** At some companies, the biggest sin a manager can commit is not knowing the answer to a boss's question. So everyone naturally overprepares for every meeting, wasting thousands of hours anticipating the questions never asked.

- Celebrate calculated risk taking, so long as the company learns from the experiment. Learn from the book *Superforecasting* about the principles of good risk management.[5] Use data and logic rather than sentiment and intuition. Keep track of where you and others came to right or wrong conclusions. Think in terms of probabilities, and test your assumptions rigorously. When you can, use test-and-learn approaches to eliminate unknowns and reduce the uncertainty.

- Modify your talent systems to find, develop, and promote people who live—and who inspire—behaviors like these. "A company's actual values," says the famous Netflix HR playbook, "are shown by who gets rewarded, promoted, or let go." Defining the behavioral signature you want (see chapter 4) is an essential part of such a system.

Throughout this book, we have argued that organizations must bring about change on both the enterprise and individual levels. Individuals affect organizations and organizations shape individuals. This is especially true of culture. Culture emerges from the cumulative behaviors of individuals, but that behavior is greatly influenced by a company's purpose, values, beliefs, and customary ways of working. The prescriptions in this chapter for building a high-performance, high-engagement culture require a great deal of interpretation and adaptation to the unique circumstances and strategy of your company. They also must be adapted to the mix of people who make up your organization.

But the need for tailoring shouldn't obscure the fundamental message. Chances are, an ownership mindset and a hunger for engagement are lying dormant under your organization's bureaucracies and management layers. Build a culture that fosters this mindset and satisfies this hunger, and you will be repaid a hundred times over by the discretionary energy and enthusiasm that you unleash.

THREE WAYS TO BUILD OR RESTORE A WINNING CULTURE

- *Raise the strategic ambition and recenter your company's purpose* in a customer- or socially focused mission. Ask yourself whether you can see your company's purpose come to life every day in your employees' actions.

- *Reawaken the ownership mindset and performance orientation* through "constructive disruptions" at moments of truth, both the symbolic and the routine. Reinforce the behaviors you want with feedback systems and consequence-based performance-management systems.

- *Reset the company's operating model, especially its ways of working and talent systems, to embed the change.* Renew your talent acquisition strategy, leadership behavioral signature, and talent-management systems to attract difference makers. Ask yourself whether you are encouraging culture-strengthening or culture-weakening behaviors.

EPILOGUE

The Virtuous Circle

An organization's productive power may well be its most important strategic asset. Consider just three of the challenges large companies face these days. Taken together, they constitute a kind of perfect storm for management teams seeking sustainable growth. And they can't be addressed effectively without a highly productive organization.

One challenge, of course, is the business cycle. We don't have a crystal ball, so we can't predict what phase of the cycle the world will be in when you read these words. But executives will always be confronted with the possibility—or the reality—of downturns. Since 1919, according to National Bureau of Economic Research data, business cycles have averaged less than six years in duration, trough to trough. The shortest has lasted less than three years, the longest more than ten.[1] Companies that fail to prepare can face catastrophic consequences. Just ask any real estate developer or lender in Las Vegas or Miami how it felt to be caught without a chair when the music stopped abruptly in 2008.

While no organization can completely insulate itself from the business cycle, companies with highly productive workforces can weather downturns better than their less productive competitors. When our partners at Bain & Company examined companies' performance in times of turbulence, they discovered that those with the highest productivity going into a downturn usually exited the downturn in a stronger market position. Often these companies were able to take advantage of weaker rivals, expanding their market share in the down cycle and maintaining it in the following upturn.[2]

An organization's productive power can also help it confront a second challenge: the possibility of a long-term decline in overall productivity. This "secular stagnation" hypothesis is hotly debated by academic and business economists, and in any event, its relevance will vary greatly from country to country and from one industry to another. But some of the statistics are hard to ignore. Economists define total factor productivity as the difference between the rate of GDP growth and the contributions made by growth in capital and labor; essentially, it's a measure of the effects of innovation and technical progress. In his book *The Rise and Fall of American Growth*, Northwestern University professor Robert Gordon observes that high total factor productivity is the exception rather than the rule—and that the metric has been nearly 40 percent lower in the last five decades (except for 1996 to 2004) than it was in the eight decades before 1972. Does that mean low total factor productivity going forward? No one knows. Still, CEOs in many industries would be foolish to discount the possibility of sluggish innovation in future years.[3]

If innovation can't be counted on to generate continued productivity growth, human capital management matters a great deal. The quality of each organization's people will determine its baseline level of performance; the better the talent, the higher the baseline. How effectively companies team, lead, and deploy that talent will determine whether they can keep their productivity growing. No exogenous factor is going to do it for them.

The third challenge is one we have mentioned frequently in this book: the superabundance of financial capital. Capital superabundance stems in large measure from demographic trends that have produced a global economy of peak savers. Our colleagues at Bain's Macro Trends Group estimate that the age group with the greatest net savings—forty-five- to fifty-nine-year-olds—will continue to expand until roughly 2040. So too much capital will be chasing too few good ideas for at least another couple of decades.[4]

Finding value-creating investments in this environment is, and will continue to be, much harder than in the past. The companies that prosper will be those that invest disproportionately in proprietary capabilities, assets, and insights. All these elements rely on great human capital, fully engaged and unconstrained by bureaucracy. As Dan Walker, former chief talent officer at Apple, notes, "Human capital is an organization's *primordial* asset."

All these challenges are beyond any company's control. But CEOs and their management teams do have control over how they respond to them, and in particular, how they manage the truly scarce resources of time, talent, and energy to keep their companies ahead of the competition. The trouble is, making the most of these scarce resources has also become more difficult in today's environment.

First, consider time management. As companies reach for growth, they frequently add new customer segments, products, services, and geographical areas. They may also attempt to buy growth through acquisitions. But the more dimensions you add to your business, the greater the complexity of your organization. Unless you are vigilant, bureaucracy-driven organizational drag will steal people's precious time and undermine the growth you are trying to stimulate. Shifting organizational structures and practices designed to foster collaboration can create a similar problem. More and more work depends on networks of individuals and empowered teams working in close collaboration, and a host of electronic tools ostensibly make such collaboration easier and cheaper. But unless you are careful, the people in your organization will come down with a bad case of collaboration overload. They'll be swamped by virtual meetings, emails, messages, and all the other methods of communication that modern technology permits.

Talent management, too, has become more challenging. Employees no longer expect to work for the same company all their lives, and the siren song of the rapidly growing company next door can be hard to resist. Indeed, many talented workers are more mobile than ever. Business networks such as LinkedIn and job databases such as Monster create greater visibility into career opportunities. Sites such as Glassdoor and Vault reveal much about what life is like inside other companies. The result is that employees are armed with more career and company information than ever before. Difference-making employees are apt to be less patient as well as more mobile, and often seek career expansion through job hopping. Lose your difference makers—or fail to deploy and team them for maximum impact—and you lose a critical competitive edge.

The management of energy is most affected by demographic and sociological trends. In the developed economies of the world, the shift from baby boomers and Gen Xers to millennials is well underway. (Millennials have already surpassed boomers as the largest living generation, according to the US Census Bureau.) Meanwhile, sluggish productivity growth and rising income inequality have dampened dreams of economic advancement for many. All this contributes to profound changes in the relationship between workers and the work they do: how they work, how much they work, and why they work in the first place—all are evolving. The workplace environment must thus meet a complex hierarchy of needs. Companies that can address those needs effectively will tap into the discretionary energy of their workforce, with a corresponding impact on relative productivity. Build a company and culture that drive performance and engagement and you will re-recruit your difference makers every day. Fail to do so and your most talented employees will head for the exits.

So managing these scarce resources is hard. But what makes the considerable effort worthwhile is the fact that each element reinforces the others, creating a virtuous circle that leaves competitors in the dust. That is what the outliers we have described in this book have tapped into.

The spinning flywheel

In this book, we have described three different elements of an organization: its time, talent, and energy. But the three elements interact, and the actions you take in one area will inevitably have an impact on the others. It helps to think of the organization as a spinning flywheel, and the actions that leaders take as speed boosts for the flywheel or, conversely, sand in the gears (see figure E-1).

FIGURE E-1

The flywheel of organizational performance

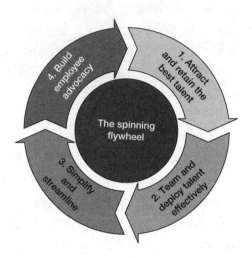

Source: Bain & Company

Here's how the flywheel works. The quality of a company's workforce sets the baseline for its productive power. A workforce composed of great talent can produce more than one made up of average or mediocre employees. Teaming and deployment act as a force multiplier, increasing the organization's productive power. Lean organizations, free from bureaucracy, allow employees to get more done, with less wasted time. If the work has a clear purpose, one that employees value, more of the workforce will be engaged. And if the company's leaders see their job not just as managing tasks but as inspiring their teams, employees will devote still more discretionary energy to the company, its customers, and the community it serves. Under these conditions, the flywheel spins quickly, unencumbered by bureaucracy and fueled by the productive power of the organization.

A holistic approach, the kind we are advocating in this book, reduces the flywheel's resistance, lowering organizational drag. It also powers up the flywheel, adding momentum as each element reinforces the others.

- **Time.** Reducing organizational drag and streamlining the organization have the direct impact of increasing a company's productive power. Fewer impediments get in the way of accomplishing great things. Organizations that are free of bureaucracy often have higher levels of workforce engagement. Word spreads, and talented workers become anxious to enlist.

- **Talent.** An organization with more difference makers in the roles where they can have the biggest impact is more productive. As the company's A-level players are teamed with others and deployed selectively, productive power increases geometrically. Equally important, talented workers don't tolerate bureaucracy or waste. Organizational drag is lower. Great talent inspires others, encouraging coworkers to bring more discretionary energy to work every day.

- **Energy.** Energized employees get more done with less. Those who are inspired get even more done. These employees also create better customer experiences, particularly in service industries. Moreover, companies with high levels of employee engagement gain a reputation as great places to work. Acquiring and retaining great talent becomes easier.

Each of the elements of productive power—time, talent, and energy—interacts with the others, enabling a company to accomplish extraordinary things. Imagine some examples. If you have an engaged and inspired workforce, these employees become your strongest advocates, not just to customers but to future employees. They provide referrals not in hopes of receiving some bounty but because they know the company, believe in it, and want their friends to work there. Research by Dr. John Sullivan & Associates suggests that employee referrals lead to more and higher-quality applicants, a better applicant-to-hire ratio, lower costs, and longer employee retention.[5] JetBlue, for instance, hires many of its customer service reps from among the community of stay-at-home mothers—many of them Mormon—in Salt Lake City. Many know each other. And Google has made a science of encouraging employee referrals. Rather than just asking for generic referrals, for example, it gets very specific. "We asked Googlers whom they would recommend for specific roles," writes HR director Laszlo Bock in his recent book, *Work Rules*. "Who is the best finance person you ever worked with? Who is the best developer in the Ruby programming language?" He adds, "Breaking down a huge question ('Do you know anyone we should hire?') into lots of small, manageable ones ('Do you know anyone who would be a good salesperson in New York?') garners us more, higher-quality referrals." Referrals increased by one-third when the company began using these techniques.[6]

Getting great talent in the door is easier in companies that have built a culture of engagement and ownership. Once they're on board, they also find it easier to perform well in teams. At Bain & Company, we have been able to create a culture that attracts high-quality recruits, generates a great deal of engagement and inspiration, and leads to high performance among our teams. Our success is reflected in leading many third-party "best places to work" lists—for example, Glassdoor, Vault, and *Consulting* magazine. Advocacy has increased over time, and that has boosted the results of our recruitment efforts. We also find that the talented people our firm hires have little patience for organizational impediments. They pressure leaders to eliminate bureaucracy and stream-line interactions. They push for effective ways of collaborating with their coworkers (and they don't assess the value of a meeting based on the quality of the cookies or sandwiches served). As a result, there are fewer pointless meetings, unnecessary emails, or frivolous IMs. Anything that gets in the way of efficiently executing Bain's customer mission is challenged and changed. And this challenge does not come from the top down; often it is the least tenured person who speaks up. The level of organizational drag plummets.

Just about all of the companies that we have highlighted in this book find a degree of synergy between the organizational elements, synergy that amps up the velocity of the flywheel. Engaged employees help companies simplify their operations. Cutting down on time wasters encourages a more productive culture. It's an organizational virtuous circle rather than the vicious cycle in which so many companies find themselves trapped. And it enables companies to do things they never thought possible.

It has never been more important for CEOs and senior leaders to manage the time, talent, and energy of their workforce. Competitive success, even survival, may depend on it. Our hope is that some of the ideas we've shared in this book will be a helpful guide for overcoming organizational drag at your company and unleashing your team's productive power. It will be the key to winning in the decades ahead.

ACKNOWLEDGMENTS

A book like this one involves contributions from many people.

First and foremost, we would like to thank our partners and colleagues at Bain & Company, who have helped us develop the ideas expressed in these pages. One of the joys of working at Bain is that we all continue to learn so much from each other. In particular, we're grateful to the members of the firm's editorial board—Wendy Miller, Paul Cichocki, Rob Markey, Patrick Litre, Phil Schefter, James Root, and Alan Bird. This group read early drafts of the manuscript on planes and over long weekends and helped us shape and refine our message. We valued this input enormously.

Our research team—Ludovica Mottura, Shih-Yu Wang, Bart van den Akker, Elizabeth Schlossberg, and Joanna Zhou—contributed in countless ways to the preparation of this book. They kept us honest, and they kept the trains running on time—no small feat with a project of this magnitude. Without their commitment and focus, we might still be debating early drafts.

Our editor, Melinda Adams Merino, and the entire team at Harvard Business Review Press encouraged us to take on this project and have guided us along the way. They constructively challenged our insights and pushed us at all the right times. The book is much stronger as a result. HBRP has been a beacon of integrity and innovation in business publishing over the years, and we're proud to be associated with it.

The dedicated team at the Economist Intelligence Unit was instrumental in helping us prepare and execute the survey research at the heart of this book. We appreciated their professionalism and ability to translate our ideas into a practical and informative questionnaire.

Our in-house editors, Paul Judge and John Case, took our occasionally cumbersome prose and turned it into something worth reading. If you find our presentation clear, concise, and interesting, much of the credit should go to them.

Our families—Bob Camp, Karen Salmon, and Aidan, Chloe, Celeste, and Marcus Garton—were endlessly patient, tolerating and even encouraging our obsessions and our nights-and-weekends hours over the many months that it took to complete the manuscript.

Finally, no acknowledgments would be complete without a hearty thank-you to the many clients that we have been privileged to serve over the years. If we have anything to offer them in this book, it is only fitting, because we have learned so much from all of them.

NOTES

Uncited quotations and other factual material are taken from interviews conducted by the authors or by other Bain & Company partners.

Prologue

1. Karen Harris, Andrew Schwedel, and Austin Kimson, "A World Awash in Money," *Bain Report*, November 14, 2012, http://www.bain.com/publications/articles/a-world-awash-in-money.aspx.

2. Patty McCord, "How Netflix Reinvented HR," *Harvard Business Review*, January–February 2014, https://hbr.org/2014/01/how-netflix-reinvented-hr.

3. Bill Taylor, "How One Company's Turnaround Came from the Heart," *Harvard Business Review*, March 30, 2010, https://hbr.org/2010/03/how-one-copmanys-turnaround.

4. Christiane Correa, *Dream Big: How the Brazilian Trio Behind 3G Capital—Jorge Paulo Lemann, Marcel Telles and Beto Sicupira—Acquired Anheuser-Busch, Burger King and Heinz* (Rio de Janeiro: Sextante, 2014).

Chapter 1

1. Bureau of Labor Statistics, "Productivity and Costs by Industry: Selected Service-Providing Industries, 2015," Long run labor productivity, unit labor costs, and related data, Table 2, http://www.bls.gov/news.release/prin2.nr0.htm.

2. Tom Monahan, "The Hard Evidence: Business Is Slowing Down," *Fortune*, January 28, 2016, http://fortune.com/2016/01/28/business-decision-making-project-management.

3. Andrew Hill, "Business: How to Topple Bureaucracy," *Financial Times*, April 14, 2016, http://on.ft.com/264hkWx.

Chapter 2

1. Andrew Grove, *Computer Decisions* 16 (1984): 126.
2. Michael C. Mankins, Chris Brahm, and Greg Caimi, "Your Scarcest Resource," *Harvard Business Review*, May 2014, https://hbr .org/2014/05/your-scarcest-resource.
3. Michael C. Mankins, "This Weekly Meeting Took Up 300,000 Hours a Year," *Harvard Business Review*, April 29, 2014, https://hbr .org/2014/04/how-a-weekly-meeting-took-up-300000-hours-a-year.
4. Adele Peters, "Why Sweden Is Shifting to a 6-Hour Workday," *Fast Company* Co.Exist, September 29, 2015, http://www.fastcoexist .com/3051448/why-sweden-is-shifting-to-a-6-hour-work-day.
5. Walter Isaacson, *Steve Jobs* (New York: Simon & Schuster, 2011).
6. Ryan Fuller, "Quantify How Much Time Your Company Wastes," *Harvard Business Review*, May 28, 2014, https://hbr .org/2014/05/quantify-how-much-time-your-company-wastes.
7. Marcia W. Blenko, Paul Rogers, and Michael C. Mankins, *Decide and Deliver: Five Steps to Breakthrough Performance in Your Organization* (Boston: Harvard Business Review Press, 2010).

Chapter 3

1. Mark Gottfredson and Michael C. Mankins, "Four Paths to a Focused Organization," *Bain Brief*, January 15, 2014, http://www .bain.com/publications/articles/four-paths-to-a-focused-organization .aspx.
2. See "Driving the Strategic Agenda in the New Work Environment," CEB, 2015, https://www.cebglobal.com/content/dam/ cebglobal/us/EN/talent-management/workforce-surveys/pdfs/ CEB-Survey-Solutions.pdf. The quote from Brian Kropp appears in Rachel Feintzeig, "So Busy at Work, No Time to Do the Job," *Wall Street Journal*, June 28, 2016, http://www.wsj.com/articles/ so-busy-at-work-no-time-to-do-the-job-1467130588.
3. Mike Myatt, "Span of Control—5 Things Every Leader Should Know," *Forbes*, November 5, 2012, http://www.forbes.com/ sites/mikemyatt/2012/11/05/span-of-control-5-things-every- leader-should-know.
4. Michael C. Mankins, "The True Cost of Hiring Yet Another Manager," *Harvard Business Review*, June 2, 2014, https://hbr .org/2014/06/the-true-cost-of-hiring-yet-another-manager.

5. Marcia W. Blenko, Eric Garton, and Ludovica Mottura, "Winning Operating Models That Convert Strategy to Results," *Bain Brief*, December 10, 2014, http://www.bain.com/publications/articles/winning-operating-models-that-convert-strategy-to-results.aspx.

6. Torsten Lichtenau, John Smith, and Sophie Horrocks, "Tackling Complexity: How to Create Simple and Effective Organizations," *Bain Brief*, June 17, 2015, http://www.bain.com/publications/articles/tackling-complexity-how-to-create-simple-and-effective-organizations.aspx.

7. Paul Rogers and Marcia W. Blenko, "Who Has the D?: How Clear Decision Roles Enhance Organizational Performance," *Harvard Business Review*, January 2006, https://hbr.org/2006/01/who-has-the-d-how-clear-decision-roles-enhance-organizational-performance.

Chapter 4

1. Michael C. Mankins, Alan Bird, and James Root, "Making Star Teams Out of Star Players," *Harvard Business Review*, January–February 2013, https://hbr.org/2013/01/ making-star-teams-out-of-star-players.

2. Kip Tindell, interview by Adam Bryant, "Three Good Hires? He'll Pay More for One Who's Great," *New York Times*, March 13, 2010, http://www.nytimes.com/2010/03/14/business/14corners.html?_r=0.

3. Steve Jobs, interview by Bob Cringely, "Steve Jobs The Lost Interview," YouTube, February 24, 2015, https://www.youtube.com/watch?v=U-rA-LWamoI.

4. R. I. M. Dunbar, "Coevolution of Neocortical Size, Group Size, and Language in Humans," *Behavioral and Brain Sciences* 16.4 (1993): 681–735.

5. Rachel Feintzeig, "Are Companies Good at Picking Stars?," *Wall Street Journal*, June 16, 2014, http://www.wsj.com/articles/are-companies-any-good-at-picking-stars-1434486106.

6. Walter Mischel and Yuichi Shoda, "A Cognitive-Affective System Theory of Personality: Reconceptualizing Situations, Dispositions, Dynamics, and Invariance in Personality Structure," *Psychology Today*, April 1995.

7. Christiane Correa, *Dream Big: How the Brazilian Trio Behind 3G Capital—Jorge Paulo Lemann, Marcel Telles and Beto Sicupira—*

Acquired Anheuser-Busch, Burger King and Heinz (Rio de Janeiro: Sextante, 2014).

8. Kenneth P. De Meuse, Guangrong Dai, George S. Hallenbeck, and King Yii Tang, "Using Learning Agility to Identify High Potentials around the World," Korn Ferry Institute Research Study, 2009.

9. O. G. Selfridge, "Pandemonium: A Paradigm for Learning," National Physical Laboratory Symposium No. 10, November 1958.

10. Reid Hoffman, Ben Casnocha, and Chris Yeh, *The Alliance: Managing Talent in the Networked Age* (Boston: Harvard Business Review Press, 2014).

Chapter 5

1. Michael C. Mankins, Alan Bird, and James Root, "Making Star Teams Out of Star Players," *Harvard Business Review*, January–February 2013, https://hbr.org/2013/01/making-star-teams-out-of-star-players.

2. NASA Associate Deputy Administrator for Policy, "Falcon 9 Launch Vehicle NAFCOM Cost Estimates," August 2011, https://www.nasa.gov/pdf/586023main_8-3-11_NAFCOM.pdf.

3. Walter Isaacson, *Steve Jobs* (New York: Simon & Schuster, 2011).

4. Julia Zorthian, "How *Toy Story* Changed Movie History," *Time*, November 19, 2015, http://time.com/4118006/20-years-toy-story-pixar.

5. "NASCAR Pit Crew," *Sports Science*, Season 4, Episode 33.

6. Matthew Yglesias, "Who's the Boss?" Slate, October 12, 2012, http://www.slate.com/articles/business/small_business/2012/10/the_value_of_a_good_boss_stanford_researchers_show_the_economic_value_of.html.

7. Edward P. Lazear, Kathryn L. Shaw, and Christopher T. Stanton, "The Value of Bosses," National Bureau of Economic Research, August 2012.

8. Ning Li, Helen H. Zhao, Sheryl L. Walter, Xin-An Zhang, and Jia Yu, "Achieving More with Less: Extra Milers' Behavioral Influence in Teams," *Journal of Applied Psychology* 100.4 (July 2015): 1025–1039.

9. Kurt Eichenwald, "Microsoft's Lost Decade," *Vanity Fair*, August 2012, http://www.vanityfair.com/news/business/2012/08/microsoft-lost-mojo-steve-ballmer.

10. Rob Cross, Reb Rebele, and Adam Grant, "Collaborative Overload," *Harvard Business Review*, January–February 2016, https://hbr.org/2016/01/collaborative-overload.

Chapter 6

1. Zeynep Ton, *The Good Jobs Strategy: How the Smartest Companies Invest in Employees to Lower Costs and Boost Profits* (New York: Houghton Mifflin Harcourt, 2014).

2. Daniel Pink, *Drive: The Surprising Truth About What Motivates Us* (New York: Riverhead Books, 2011).

3. Jennifer Robin, "The Path that Builds Trust," Great Place to Work blog, August 29, 2013, http://www.greatplacetowork.com/events-and-insights/blogs-and-news/2245-one-rule#sthash.EorfKmNT.dpbs.

4. Humayun Khan, "How Nordstrom Made Its Brand Synonymous With Customer Service (and How You Can Too)," Shopify, May 2, 2016, https://www.shopify.com/retail/119531651-how-nordstrom-made-its-brand-synonymous-with-customer-service-and-how-you-can-too.

5. Christian Conte, "Nordstrom Customer Service Tales Not Just Legend," *Jacksonville Business Journal*, September 7, 2012, http://www.bizjournals.com/jacksonville/blog/retail_radar/2012/09/nordstrom-tales-of-legendary-customer.html.

6. Henrik Kniberg, "Spotify Engineering Culture (parts 1 & 2)," Spotify Labs blog, March 27, 2014, https://labs.spotify.com/2014/03/27/spotify-engineering-culture-part-1.

Chapter 7

1. Louis V. Gerstner Jr., *Who Says Elephants Can't Dance? Inside IBM's Historic Turnaround* (New York: HarperBusiness, 2012), 181.

2. "Futurestep survey: organizational culture and employer brand are top competitive advantages when recruiting talent," Korn Ferry Futurestep blog, June 16, 2015, http://www.futurestep.com/

news/futurestep-survey-organizational-culture-and-employer-brand-are-top-competitive-advantages-when-recruiting-talent.

3. Founder's Mentality is a registered trademark of Bain & Company, Inc.

4. Chris Zook and James Allen, *The Founder's Mentality: How to Overcome the Predictable Crises of Growth* (Boston: Harvard Business Review Press, 2016).

5. Philip E. Tetlock and Dan Gardner, *Superforecasting: The Art and Science of Prediction* (New York: Crown, 2015).

Epilogue

1. National Bureau of Economic Research, "US Business Cycle Expansions and Contractions," September 20, 2010, http://www .nber.org/cycles.html.

2. Darrell K. Rigby and Mark Gottfredson, "Winning in Turbulence: The Power of Managing Complexity," *Harvard Business Review*, February 23, 2009, https://hbr.org/2009/02/winning-in-turbulence-the-powe.

3. Robert J. Gordon, *The Rise and Fall of American Growth: The U.S. Standard of Living Since the Civil War* (Princeton, NJ: Princeton University Press, 2016).

4. Karen Harris, Andrew Schwedel, and Austin Kimson, "A World Awash in Money," *Bain Report*, November 14, 2012, http:// www.bain.com/publications/articles/a-world-awash-in-money.aspx.

5. Dr. John Sullivan, "10 Compelling Numbers That Reveal the Power of Employee Referrals," Eremedia, May 7, 2012, http://www.eremedia.com/ere/10-compelling-numbers-that-reveal-the-power-of-employee-referrals.

6. Lazlo Bock, *Work Rules!: Insights from Google That Will Transform How You Live and Lead* (New York: Twelve, 2015).

INDEX

Page numbers ending in an *f* indicate a figure. Page numbers ending in *t* indicate a table.

ABOUT THE AUTHORS

MICHAEL MANKINS is a partner in Bain's San Francisco office and head of the firm's organization practice in the Americas. He is coauthor of *Decide & Deliver: Five Steps to Breakthrough Performance in Your Organization* (Harvard Business Review Press, 2010) and *The Value Imperative: Managing for Superior Shareholder Returns* (Free Press, 1994). His writings and ideas have appeared in numerous *Harvard Business Review* articles as well as in the *Wall Street Journal*, *Financial Times*, *New York Times*, and many other publications. He has also been a featured speaker at conferences conducted by *Harvard Business Review*, *Business Week*, *CFO Magazine*, *Directors & Boards*, and other organizations. In 2006, *Consulting* magazine named Michael one of the year's "Top 25 most influential consultants."

ERIC GARTON is a partner in Bain's Chicago office, leader of the firm's global organization practice, and a senior member of the consumer products and industrial goods and services practices. Since joining Bain in 1997, Eric has focused his time on working with global companies undergoing significant organizational transformation.